# British Monsters
## Volume One
### 15 Terrifying Tales of Britain's Most Horrific Serial Killers

# Robert Keller

Please Leave Your Review of This Book At
http://bit.ly/kellerbooks

ISBN-13: 978-1535211093
ISBN-10: 1535211091

© 2016 by Robert Keller

robertkellerauthor.com

All rights reserved.

No part of this publication may be copied or reproduced in any format, electronic or otherwise, without the prior, written consent of the copyright holder and publisher. This book is for informational and entertainment purposes only and the author and publisher will not be held responsible for the misuse of information contain herein, whether deliberate or incidental.

Much research, from a variety of sources, has gone into the compilation of this material. To the best knowledge of the author and publisher, the material contained herein is factually correct. Neither the publisher, nor author will be held responsible for any inaccuracies.

# Table of Contents

Peter Manuel ..................................................................................... 5

George Joseph Smith ..................................................................... 15

Donald Neilson ............................................................................... 29

John Reginald Christie ................................................................... 35

John Duffy and David Mulcahy ..................................................... 51

Peter Tobin ..................................................................................... 63

Amelia Dyer ................................................................................... 67

Ian Brady and Myra Hindley .......................................................... 79

Graham Young ............................................................................... 93

Robert Black ................................................................................ 107

William Palmer ............................................................................ 121

Burke and Hare ............................................................................ 127

Bruce Peter George Lee ............................................................... 139

Harold Shipman ........................................................................... 145

Jack the Stripper .......................................................................... 157

# Peter Manuel

## The Beast of Birkenshaw

*"I am the foulest beast on earth... A reptile in disguise."* – Peter Manuel

Peter Manuel is Scotland's most notorious serial killer, a brutal psychopath who claimed at least 8 victims (and possibly as many as 18) in an orgy of violence between 1956 and 1958. A habitual criminal from the age of 11, Manuel graduated from burglary to rape to murder, killing male and female, young and old with equal alacrity. "You can have various aspects to a psychopathic personality," Dr. Richard Goldberg of Aberdeen University said in discussing his case. "What is really fascinating about Manuel is that he ticks every box."

Manuel was born in New York City on March 13, 1927, the second of three children. His parents, Samuel and Bridget, had immigrated to America in the 1920s. But his father's ill heath had forced them to return to Scotland in 1932. On their return, they settled briefly in Motherwell before moving south of the border to Coventry.

Manuel struggled to fit in at school and was in trouble from an early age. In 1938, aged just 11, he broke into a chapel and stole money from the collection box. Later that same year he was caught burglarizing a shop and a house. Those offenses landed him in a reform school, but he habitually escaped to commit burglaries in the area. In October 10, 1941, he broke into a house and threatened the householder with an axe. A year later, during yet another break-in, he struck a woman on the head while she slept, causing concussion and hemorrhage. The woman was hospitalized for some time, while Manuel simply shrugged his shoulders and pled guilty.

By now, the education system was at a loss as to what to do with Manuel. At age 15, he was already a habitual criminal and no amount of punishment seemed to have any effect on him.

His next offense was more serious than breaking and entering, he was charged with indecently assaulting the wife of one of the school staff. After hitting the woman on the head with a stick of wood, Manuel dragged her into some trees where he ripped off her clothes and tried to rape her. She was found later in a semi-conscious state. She'd suffered a concussion and required eight stitches to her head. Her nose and collarbone had also been broken in the attack.

Manuel again pled guilty. He was also charged with housebreaking and malicious damage to property after it was discovered that he'd burgled a house and destroyed bedding and clothing by cutting. He'd also scattered foodstuffs and cigarette butts around the scene, something that would become a trademark of his future crimes.

After these latest offenses, Manuel was held for a month in Leeds Prison. His father requested that he be transferred to a reformatory in Scotland, but this was refused. Instead, he'd be incarcerated for two years at a juvenile detention center in Yorkshire. Yet even now, he was unrepentant. He continued to abscond, continued to commit crimes. The school was glad to see the back of him in 1946.

Manuel, now 18, moved to Lanarkshire, Scotland, where his parents lived. He was immediately in trouble again. In February 1946, he was caught breaking into a house. While out on bail for that offense, he assaulted three women, raping one of them.

On June 25, 1946, he was sentenced to eight years in Peterhead Prison for the rape. While incarcerated in Peterhead, Manuel expressed his disgust at the way he'd been treated by the courts. He asked to be supplied with various law books and spent much of his time reading up on the Scottish legal system.

But Manuel didn't spend all of his time reading. He was a persistent troublemaker described by prison officers as a 'very unpleasant type of prisoner.' After an incident in 1950, in which he smashed 30 windowpanes and threatened two officers with glass shards, he was examined by a psychiatrist who concluded that he was an 'aggressive psychopath.' The doctor went on to add: "It is doubtful whether, even at the beginning of his sentence, any constructive work could have been done with him."

Nonetheless, Manuel was released from his sentence a year early and returned to the family home in Birkenshaw, Lanarkshire. For a while, it looked as though he was trying to go straight. He found a job as a laborer with the Scottish Gas Board and in the autumn of 1954 started dating a girl named Anne O'Hara, a conductress on the bus he took to work. The following year the couple got engaged, but the relationship floundered and eventually ended over Manuel's refusal to attend church.

Shortly after Anne called off the engagement Manuel was in trouble again, this time for indecent assault. He defended himself at trial and was acquitted. Not long after, he graduated to murder.

On the afternoon of January 4, 1956, the body of 17-year-old Anne Knielands was found in woodland adjacent to a golf course at East Kilbride. She'd been brutally battered about the head and evidence suggested that she'd been chased for some distance before her killer had eventually caught up with her and bludgeoned her to death. Although she hadn't been raped, semen stains on her clothing suggested that her killer had masturbated over her corpse.

As they initiated their enquiries, the police learned that a team of Scottish Gas Board employees had been working in the area over the last few days and that one of them had scratch marks on his face. That man was Peter Manuel, already known to officers as a violent offender. Manuel was questioned and items of his clothing taken away for forensic examination. He denied any knowledge of the crime, claiming he'd gotten the scratches in a bar fight and had been at home on the night of the murder. Manuel's father corroborated his alibi, and when the tests on his clothes came back negative, the police began focusing their attention on other suspects. One officer, though, Chief Inspector William Muncie, continued to regard Manuel as the man most likely to have killed Anne Knielands

Two months after the Knielands murder, the police got a tip-off that a robbery was going to take place at a colliery in Blantyne. Manuel was named as one of the two men involved. A trap was laid and although Manuel managed to escape, he left incriminating evidence at the scene and was soon under arrest.

He was arraigned at Hamilton Sheriff's Court where he was granted bail. While Manuel was awaiting trial, the police were called to the scene of two burglaries, both bearing Manuel's unique signature - food and cigarette butts scattered across the scene.

Then, on the morning of September 17, officers were called to a bungalow in Fennsbank Avenue, High Burnside, close to the scene of the two earlier break-ins. Inside they found the bodies of Marion Watt, 45, her 16-year-old daughter Vivienne, and Margaret Brown, Mrs. Watt's sister. All three had been shot dead at close range.

There was spilled food and discarded cigarette butts at the scene, leading police to immediately suspect Manuel. Detectives were dispatched to his home with a search warrant, but they turned up nothing incriminating. Manual also refused to answer any of their questions and the officers left frustrated.

There'd soon be a new suspect anyway, Mrs. Watt's husband, William. He'd been away on a fishing trip in Argyll at the time of the murders, but the investigators suspected he had driven home from the hotel where he was staying, committed the murders, and then returned to Lochgilphead to continue his holiday. There were plenty of flaws in the theory, but on September 27, Watt was arrested and charged with the murders of his wife, daughter and sister-in-law. He would be held at Barlinnie Prison for 67 days before being released when detectives eventually admitted they had the wrong man.

Also incarcerated at Barlinnie during that time was Peter Manuel, just starting an 18-month sentence for the attempted robbery at the Blantyre Colliery. Manuel seemed very interested in the Watt case, even asking William Watt's solicitor for a meeting at which he claimed to know the identity of the killer. He refused to give a name, but it was soon obvious that Manuel knew more than he should about the murders. The solicitor passed his suspicions on to the police, but while they now believed that Manuel was their man, they had no hard evidence against him.

Manuel was released from Barlinnie in November 1957. Within days of his release, he moved to Newcastle-upon-Tyne, ostensibly to find work. On December 8, 1957, a 36-year-old taxi driver named Sydney Dunn was found dead in his cab on a desolate stretch of moorland in Northumberland. He'd been shot at close range and his throat had been slit. Manuel had been in Newcastle at the time of Dunn's death but had returned to Scotland by the time the body was found. Some doubt exists as to whether or not Manuel killed Dunn. He never confessed to the murder. However, two weeks after Manuel's execution it was revealed that a button matching one of his coats was found in Dunn's cab.

On December 29, 1957, the police received a report that 17-year-old Isabelle Cooke, from Mount Vernon, had disappeared. The teenager had left home the previous evening to attend a dance and was supposed to meet up with her boyfriend at a bus stop near her Glasgow home. She never arrived. The police mounted a hunt for Isabelle and found various items of her clothing. However, there was no trace of the missing girl.

A week later, the police were called to the scene of another triple homicide. The bodies of Peter Smart, his wife Doris and the couple's 11-year-old son Michael were found in their home in Uddingston. All three victims were still in their beds. They'd been shot in the head at point-blank range, apparently while they slept.

The police were certain that Peter Manuel was responsible. Proving it, though, was another matter. Manuel had no motive and no links to the victims. No one had seen him enter the home and very little evidence was left at the scene. They decided to place Manuel under surveillance and detailed a twenty-man team to keep a watch on him. The surveillance team soon hit paydirt. They noticed that even though Manuel was unemployed, he was spending a lot of time drinking in Glasgow's bars, paying with crisp new banknotes. Following up on this clue they managed to obtain a few of these notes and took them to Peter Smart's bank. There they learned that Smart had recently made a large withdrawal to pay for a family holiday and that the banknotes

Manuel was using could be positively linked to that withdrawal. Finally, they had the evidence they needed.

Early on the morning of January 14, 1958, a little over two years since the murder of Anne Knielands, Lanarkshire police finally moved in to arrest Peter Manuel. The raid on the family home in Birkenshaw turned up additional evidence - a Kodak camera and a pair of gloves, which Manuel had given to his sister and father as Christmas gifts proved to be from one of Manuel's earlier break-ins. Manuel was arrested for housebreaking, his father for receiving stolen goods.

This was a deliberate ploy on the part of the investigation team. They knew that Manuel was very close to his family and that he would not want his father to get into trouble for something he had done. After leaving him alone in his cell for 24 hours, Manuel finally cracked. He offered detectives a deal - drop all charges against his father and he'd help them 'resolve' certain unsolved cases.

The officers eventually agreed and, with his parents present, Manuel started speaking, confessing in detail to the murders of Anne Kneilands, Marion and Vivienne Watts, Margaret Brown, and the Smart family. He also surprised officers by admitting that he killed Isabelle Cooke. That murder had not yet been connected to him. Manuel subsequently led officers to the plowed field where he'd buried Isabel's body. Asked where exactly the body was located he reportedly told officers: "I think I am standing on her."

On May 12, 1958, Manuel stood trial for murder at Glasgow's High Court. The trial was a sensation, with spectators queuing around the block for a seat in the public gallery. If they expected a spectacle, they were not disappointed with Manuel firing his lawyers and opting to conduct his own defense. All of those years behind bars studying Scottish law were put to good use as he filed a motion to have his confessions suppressed, claiming they'd been given under duress. Unfortunately for Manuel, the judge rejected his petition. The confessions stood and along with evidence about the banknotes stolen from the Smart residence, and a letter written to William Watt's solicitor, served to build a strong case against Manuel. The jury deliberated for a mere two hours and 21 minutes before finding him guilty on all charges bar the Anne Kneilands' murder (the judge had ruled that the jury should not find Manuel guilty in her case, due to lack of evidence).

Manuel was sentenced to hang and remanded to Barlinnie to await execution. Initially upbeat and chatty with the guards, in the days leading up to his execution, his mental condition began to deteriorate. He refused to speak and barely ate, at one point refusing food for four days. He was found on occasion lying on his cot, limbs twitching and froth coming from his mouth. He developed a shuffling gait, his body movements clumsy and ungainly. On other occasions, he'd lie on his cot groaning and whimpering.

On June 24, the Appeals Court in Edinburgh rejected his final appeal. He was returned to Barlinnie where he kept up his charade, no doubt trying to convince the authorities that he was insane. Then, on July 10, the day before his execution, he underwent another transformation. The talkative, cheerful Manuel was back.

After a last supper of fish, chips, lettuce and tomatoes, Manuel met with the prison governor for two hours, during which time he is said to have confessed to as many as 18 unsolved murders. At around 8 p.m., he had a visit from his older brother David. After David left, Manuel lay awake for most of the night. At 6.50 a.m., he heard Mass and took Holy Communion. The prison governor and executioner entered the cell at 7:58 p.m. Manuel spoke briefly with the governor, thanking him and his staff. Then he turned to the hangman and said: "Turn up the radio and I'll go quietly."

A minute later he was escorted across the gallery to the hanging shed where he was executed at 8 a.m. exactly. Manuel was buried in the prison cemetery. He was 31 years old at the time of his death.

# George Joseph Smith

## The Brides in the Bath Murderer

*"I may be a bit peculiar but I am certainly no murderer!"* – George Joseph Smith

George Joseph Smith was born in Bethnal Green, London on January 11, 1872. His father was an insurance agent - a far from lucrative trade in those days – and the family struggled to make ends meet. From an early age, Smith and his siblings were left mainly to the streets, and for Smith, that meant a career in petty thievery. At the age of just nine, he was arrested for stealing fruit from a vendor and was sent to a reformatory. For the next eight years, Smith was subjected to the harsh brutality of the Victorian reform system, a grounding that no doubt helped to shape the calculating killer he'd later become.

Released in 1888, Smith soon engulfed himself in a life of petty larceny. He served a week in jail in 1890 for theft, and six months in prison the following year for stealing a bicycle. A break from his criminal career followed in the early 1890's when he enlisted in the army. His postings over the next few years taking him overseas.

By 1896, Smith was back in Britain and ready for a new vocation, that of a dapper swindler. He'd always been a handsome man, but the years in the army had transformed his once scrawny body into a lean muscular frame. He had also learned, by observing his officers, how to present himself as a gentleman. A few cheap suits and some cut-price cologne and George Joseph Smith was ready to do business. Except, he wasn't calling himself Smith anymore, he was now George Baker.

Smith's scheme was simple. He targeted young, unsophisticated, servant girls wooing them with his suave line of talk, over time building up a virtual harem of adoring accomplices. He then got these swooning housemaids to compile an inventory of valuables in the mansions where they were employed. Smith would scan the lists, picking out the items he wanted. The maids would then steal them for him. It worked perfectly for a time, allowing Smith to live quite comfortably and even to start a small savings account. But it was all undone when one of his lovers, jealous of the attention he was paying another, informed on him. Smith was promptly arrested and sent to prison for a year.

Upon his release, Smith moved to Leicester and with his savings opened a small sweet shop. While he was in Leicester he met Caroline Thornhill, and the couple was married in 1898, Smith using the alias, George Oliver Love. They moved into the back of Smith's candy store, but the business had already started to fail and once Caroline's small savings account was depleted, he told her he was leaving. Caroline begged him not to go and Smith eventually acquiesced. There was a condition, though, they were to return to London, where Caroline was to find work as a maid. Smith soon revived his earlier scheme, with his wife now working as his accomplice. Soon the money was rolling in, Smith meticulously recording each larceny in a journal, a habit he'd maintain throughout his life.

While Caroline continued her thievery on his behalf, Smith began venturing further afield, visiting the seaside towns along the south coast. He passed himself off as an antiques dealer and in this guise wooed and robbed any number of gullible women. He may even have married a few of them because Smith by now saw bigamy as his road to riches.

However, he was soon to suffer a setback with his real wife. Caroline was caught stealing from one of her employers. She immediately fingered Smith as the mastermind behind the scheme and he was arrested. He received the maximum two-year prison term for receiving stolen goods, emerging in 1902, by which time Caroline had flown the coop to Canada.

Unperturbed by this setback, Smith fell immediately back into his old routine, wooing, marrying, robbing and deserting lonely spinsters. Exactly how many gullible women he duped in this way is unknown, but he accumulated enough money to buy a second hand store in Bristol. It was in Bristol that he met Edith Peglar, marrying her in July 1908, under his real name. Edith was soon duped out of her life's savings, but for some reason Smith hung around until the summer of 1910, before abandoning her in a ploy he'd used before. He took her to the National Gallery, excused himself to go to the men's room and never returned.

It has never been established when Smith decided to incorporate murder into his modus operandi. Some writers have speculated that it was his relationship with Edith Pegler that pushed him in that direction. Smith felt genuine affection for Edith. It bothered him, and he was determined not to let emotions cloud his judgment. A far more likely explanation was that he hated women, hated the way they fawned over him, hated the way they were so easily duped, hated the sexual acts he was required to perform as part of his marital duties. Murder then, was a means unto an end, a payoff for what he had to endure. Whatever the truth of the matter, Smith's next wife would not live to regret falling for his charms.

In August 1910, Smith (using the alias Henry Williams) met Beatrice Constance "Bessie" Mundy, a 33-year-old spinster. Bessie was a plain-looking woman, but she had one thing that was irresistible to Smith, a £2, 500 inheritance. He quickly proposed and she accepted. Unfortunately for Smith, he hadn't done his homework. Bessie's money was controlled by her uncle, she was only allowed a weekly allowance of £8. Smith tried everything he could to get his hands on the lump sum, cajoling, threatening, even employing a solicitor. His prize after all that effort was a mere £138. The uncle stood firm on the rest.

Believing that he'd get nothing more from Bessie's inheritance, Smith sought a way out of the marriage. He accused Bessie of promiscuity and of infecting him with a venereal disease, a quite ludicrous charge. Bessie was a moral, upstanding person. The same could most certainly not be said for Smith. Nonetheless, it served as an excuse for him to desert yet another wife. He soon absconded and returned to Edith Peglar, leaving Bessie broken-hearted.

For the next two years, Smith kept up his insalubrious activities, shuttling between London and Bristol with Edith in tow. Bessie Mundy, meanwhile, moved to a boarding house in Weston-super-Mare and continued her lonely existence.

On March 14, 1912, Bessie had been out for a stroll when she returned to the house in a state of nervous excitement. She told the landlady, Mrs. Tuckett that she'd just encountered her errant husband, Henry Williams. Two years had passed since Henry had deserted his wife, cursing her for infecting him with syphilis, but he'd begged her forgiveness and, in an instant, Bessie had forgiven him.

About two hours later, Smith showed up at the boarding house and, despite Mrs. Tuckett's concerns, Bessie was soon packed and ready to go, although not before Smith had taken her to Baker & Co. Solicitors to arrange a £150 loan against her inheritance. The couple next showed up in Herne Bay where they rented a house on High Street. Smith then began putting in place his devious plan for relieving Bessie of her inheritance.

His first step was to make out a will in favor of his wife (worthless, since he had nothing to leave her). Bessie duly reciprocated, leaving all of her worldly possessions to her beloved Henry in the event of her death, thus sealing her fate. Smith moved quickly. The following day, he visited an ironmonger in the town and purchased an iron tub, haggling the price down and buying the bath on credit. On July 10, he took Bessie to visit a local physician, Dr. French. Smith insisted that his wife had suffered some kind of fit, even though Bessie had no recollection of it and said she felt fine. French examined Bessie, then gave her a bromide and sent the couple home.

A couple of days later, a frantic Smith appeared at Dr. French's rooms. "My wife has had another fit," he said. "Please come quickly." Dr. French found Bessie in a slightly dazed state but otherwise okay. He concluded that the stifling heat of the day might have brought on the episode and promised to call on Bessie later. When he returned he found her happy and in good health.

As soon as Dr. French left, Smith convinced Bessie to write a letter to her uncle. "Last Thursday night I had a bad fit," she wrote. "My husband has provided me with the very best medical men who attend me night and day. I have made a will and bequeathed all to my husband. This is only natural as I love my husband." Smith dutifully sealed the envelope and rushed it immediately into the mail.

Early on July 13, Smith woke Bessie and told her that he'd prepared a nice, hot bath for her. An hour later, a schoolboy appeared at Dr. French's rooms and handed him a note from Smith. "Can you come at once," it read. "I'm afraid my wife is dead."

Dr. French left immediately for the Williams' home where he found Bessie lying on her back in the bathtub, her head submerged, a bar of soap clutched in her hand. He lifted the corpse from the bath and attempted artificial respiration, but it was no use. Bessie had apparently suffered a fit while in the bathtub and drowned.

Of course, Smith had carefully laid the groundwork to support this ruse, so the coroner had no problem in recording a verdict of accidental death. No one seems to have considered how such a tall woman could have drowned in such a small tub.

Smith hastily arranged a funeral, haggling with the undertaker before settling on the cheapest possible coffin, not even paying for a private plot, burying Bessie instead in a communal grave. Two hours later, he hauled the bathtub to the ironmongers and insisted on a refund. Immediately after, he quit town and began proceedings to get his hands on Bessie's estate. The Mundy family tried to fight him, but in the end were forced to pay over £2, 000. Smith had Bessie's legally attested will after all.

In late August, Smith was back in Bristol, flush with more money than he'd ever had in his life. When Edith Peglar asked about the source of his newfound wealth, he said that he'd been to Canada where he'd made the money trading antiques.

Smith fancied himself as a shrewd businessman and with the proceeds of Bessie's estate he purchased 10 small houses in Bristol. He planned on building a great fortune with his ill-gotten gains, but within just a few months he'd already lost £700 on his investments. It was time for him to return to the only profession at which he was able to make money.

In October 1913, he met Alice Burnham, an overweight, 26-year-old nurse, who was immediately smitten by the dapper Smith. Her father, though, was less convinced, correctly gauging Smith's intentions. Charles Burnham was holding £100 in savings for his daughter. Smith wanted to get his hands on it.

Ever the optimist, Smith used Burnham's dislike of him to his advantage, he convinced Alice to elope with him. They were married in Portsmouth on November 4. On December 10, the newly-weds turned up in Blackpool, where they rented rooms from a Mrs. Crossley, Smith insisting that the suite must contain a bath. He then got to work harassing his wife's money out of her family. Faced with the threat of legal action, Charles Burnham reluctantly paid over the £100.

By this time, Smith had already taken out a £500 insurance policy on Alice's life. He now began his familiar routine, preparing the ground for murder. After confiding in Mrs. Crossley that his wife suffered from severe headaches he asked if the landlady might recommend a good doctor. Mrs. Crossley suggested Dr. George Billing, who examined Alice at his clinic a short while later. He found her to be in good health but thought he detected a slight heart murmur.

That night, at around 6 p.m. Smith asked Mrs. Crossley to prepare a bath for Alice. Two hours later, as the Crossley family sat down to dinner, they noticed a large stain on the ceiling and water dripping from the room above. Mrs. Crossley had just instructed her daughter to go and check on it when Smith suddenly appeared in the kitchen. He was carrying a package of eggs and said he'd been out to buy them for his and his wife's breakfast. Mrs. Crossley pointed out the stain on the ceiling, at which Smith rushed up the stairs. A moment later, he called down, "My wife will not speak to me. Quick, get Dr. Billing! He knows her! Hurry!"

When Billing arrived he found Smith in the bathroom holding his wife's head above the water. Between them, they lifted Alice's heavy body from the tub and Billing tried unsuccessfully to revive her. The coroner was called and on the advice of Dr. Billing, recorded the death as accidental drowning, noting that the deceased had suffered a heart attack while in the bath.

Later that night, Smith wrote to the insurance company, claiming the £500 on the death of his wife. With that money in hand, he returned to Bristol and Edith Peglar, telling again the story of a successful business trip to Canada.

Smith had now twice gotten away with murder. He must have thought himself invincible. In September 1914, he married Alice Reavil in Woolwich, but learning that his new wife could not be insured due to ill health, he swiftly abandoned her.

He had better luck three months later when he encountered 38-year-old Margaret Lofty, a vicar's daughter. Using the name John Lloyd, Smith hastily proposed and the love-starved Margaret readily agreed. The couple traveled to the town of Bath for the nuptials – no doubt Smith's idea of a joke. The marriage took place on December 17, 1914, whereupon Smith took out a £700 insurance policy on his wife, with the Yorkshire Insurance Co.

With the wedding completed, Lofty drew her entire savings, a sum of £20, and the couple departed for London. They found lodgings at a boarding house in Highgate, run by a Mrs. Blatch. Smith made big deal about inspecting the bath before handing over the rent money. He then told Mrs. Blatch that his wife was feeling unwell and asked if she could suggest a doctor.

A short while later, the Lloyds paid a visit to Dr. Bates. He examined Margaret and found her in good health, if a little feverish. "Might she be suffering from fits?" Smith suggested. Dr. Bates said that she might, but prescribed only a mild sedative.

With his previous two murders, Smith had waited weeks before carrying through with his plan. He wasn't going to wait that long this time, not with £700 just waiting to be collected. No sooner had he and Margaret returned to their rooms that he suggested a nice, hot bath to relax her.

Mrs. Blatch drew the bath for Margaret at 7:30 p.m. Minutes later, she heard a faint splash from the bathtub and then the sound of the melodeon being played in the living room, a hymn she recognized, 'Closer My Lord To Thee.'

A while later the doorbell rang. Mrs. Blatch went to answer it and found Smith on the doorstep. He said he'd been to buy some tomatoes for his wife's dinner and had forgotten his key. He then glanced around the living room and seemed perplexed. "Isn't my wife down from her bath yet?" he asked. Mrs. Blatch answered that she hadn't seen Margaret and Smith then made an odd request – he suggested that the landlady should accompany him upstairs to fetch her.

The bathroom was in darkness, but as Smith turned on the light, Mrs. Blatch saw Margaret in the tub, her head submerged. Smith pulled her from the water and made a great show of trying to revive her. Of course, it was no use. Dr. Bates was called. He concluded that Margaret had drowned, adding that influenza, together with the heat of the bath might have caused an attack of syncope.

The coroner agreed and following a hastily arranged funeral, Smith returned to Edith Peglar in Bristol. Now all he had to do was wait for his payout of £700. It was so simple that he thought he might soon do another one.

But Smith had already made a fatal mistake. The simplicity of his murder for profit scheme, the repetitive nature of it, was about to catch up with him.

In January 1915, Charles Burnham, who'd never accepted that his daughter Alice's death had been an accident, spotted an article in the News of the World. It was about the strange and tragic death of Margaret Lofty. Burnham was astounded by the similarity to Alice's death. He clipped the article from the paper and forwarded it to the police, together with an article about his daughter's drowning. At around the same time, Joseph Crossley, husband of the landlady who'd provide Smith and Alice with lodgings, came to a similar conclusion. He too forwarded the articles to the police.

Scotland Yard must have thought there was a case to be investigated because they assigned Detective Inspector Arthur Fowler Neil to the case. Neil, known for his intellect and meticulous nature, began by inspecting the bath in which Margaret Lofty had drowned. He decided that it was impossible for a grown woman to drown in such a small tub, and came to a similar conclusion in the Alice Burnham case. During the course of his enquiries, he also learned of the death of Bessie Mundy and determined that the descriptions of the husbands in each case – Williams, Smith and Lloyd - were startlingly similar.

Next, Neil ran a check on insurance companies and found that Mrs. Lloyd had been insured by the Yorkshire Insurance Co., and that Mr. Lloyd's negotiations with that company were being handled by his attorney, W.T. Davies. Neil wasted no time in contacting the insurance company and asking them to expedite payment to Mr. Lloyd. Then he posted detectives outside Davies' London office and waited for Williams/Smith/Lloyd to show up.

At around 12:30 p.m. on February 1, 1915, Neil himself was stationed outside the lawyer's office when a man fitting Lloyd's description appeared. Neil approached, introduced himself and asked the man whether he was John Lloyd. "Yes," replied the man. Then Neil asked him whether he was also George Smith. The man vigorously denied it. However, Neil was certain that Lloyd was lying, and told him that he was taking him in for questioning on a charge of bigamy. Visibly relieved, "Lloyd" then admitted that he was George Smith.

With Smith in custody, Neil obtained exhumation orders for the bodies of Bessie Mundy, Alice Burnham and Margaret Lofty. Smith had not yet been charged with murder. First, Neil had to work out how he had killed three women and made each of their deaths look like an accident. In order to do this, he called on the services of the acclaimed pathologist, Sir Bernard Spilsbury.

However, Spilsbury found no signs of violence on the bodies, which there would surely have been if Smith had forced any of the women's heads under the water. All three women had indeed drowned and it looked like Smith would get away with it, for lack of evidence.

But Inspector Neil was not so easily bowed. He decided to re-enact the bathtub scenes, using women who were of similar height and build to the three victims but were also experienced swimmers. Using the very tubs in which the victims had died, he tried various ways to push the women's heads under water without a struggle. All failed until Neil hit on an idea. Walking to the front of the tub, he grabbed the woman's ankles and yanked them towards him. Caught by surprise, the woman's head was instantly submerged, causing her to pass out immediately.

Neil and Spilsbury quickly pulled her from the tub and spent a frantic half-hour reviving her. When the woman was sufficiently recovered she told them that the instant her head was pulled under, her nose and mouth filled with water causing her to immediately black out. At last, Neil and Spilsbury had their answer. They knew how the 'Brides in the Bath' murders had been committed.

Smith's trial began at the Old Bailey on June 22, 1915. Neil had tried to keep the investigation low-key, but word of the sensational murders had leaked out and the public galleries were full to overflowing with spectators, many of them the type of lonely, love-starved women whom Smith had preyed on.

The trial got off to a sensational start. As the judge cautioned the jury that they were about to hear a murder charge, Smith shouted out: "This is a disgrace in a Christian country! I may be a bit peculiar, but I am certainly no murderer!"

Declarations of innocence notwithstanding, the next 9 days saw a parade of witnesses making an ever more compelling case against Smith. The clincher came when Inspector Neil demonstrated how Smith had drowned his wives simply by yanking their legs in the air. Shaking with anger, Smith yelled: "That man's a villain. He should be in the dock, not me!"

Eventually, the matter went to the jury, who returned a guilty verdict after just 23 minutes of deliberation. His appeal denied, Smith was transported to Maidstone prison to await execution.

At 8 p.m. on August 13, 1915, Smith was removed from his cell and marched across the courtyard towards the gallows. As he saw the scaffold, his legs collapsed and he had to be carried the rest of the way. His arms were bound, a hood placed over his head and the noose fixed in place around his neck. "I am in terror," Smith whimpered in the moment before the trapdoor was opened.

# Donald Neilson

*The Black Panther*

Donald Neilson was born Donald Nappey in Bradford, England on August 1, 1936. As a child, and later during his military service, he was constantly teased and taunted about his surname (the word 'nappy' is the British equivalent of 'diaper'). Despite this, Neilson enjoyed his time in the army, which saw him posted to Kenya, Aden, and Cyprus. He was seriously considering a military career until his fiancé, Irene, talked him out of it.

Neilson returned to Bradford, where he started work as a carpenter. In 1955, he married Irene Tate, two years his senior. The couple's daughter, Kathryn, was born in 1960. Times were hard for the family, with Neilson struggling to earn a living at his chosen trade and also failing in attempts to start a taxi service and a security guard business. Shortly after the birth of his daughter, he changed his name by deed poll to Neilson, the name of a man from whom he'd bought a taxi cab.

Part of the reason that Neilson changed his name was to protect his daughter from the teasing and bullying he'd experienced as a child. But Neilson wasn't above bullying his own family. Neighbors would later comment on how domineering he was towards them and how poorly dressed they always were. He would also force Irene and Kathryn into participating in "war games," where they were required to dress in military clothing, camp out in the woods and "play soldiers" for his amusement.

By 1965, Neilson had had enough of living in poverty and decided to do something about it. His solution was to turn to crime, and he began a career as a successful burglar, committing over 400 break-ins without being caught. The pickings, though, were decidedly slim and in 1967 Neilson upped the ante, graduating from burglary to armed robbery.

The targets of his new crime spree were sub-post offices, the small privately run postal depots that dotted Britain at the time. These, he figured, would be lightly guarded and therefore easy pickings for a determined gunman. Between 1967 and 1972 he carried out 19 such raids in Yorkshire and Lancashire, but the cash haul was disappointing, leaving Neilson angry and embittered, and increasingly violent in the commission of his robberies. Eventually, it led him to murder.

In early February 1972, Neilson broke into a post office in Heywood, Lancashire. The postmaster, Leslie Richardson, lived in an apartment above the store and went downstairs to investigate after hearing a noise. There he encountered a masked man, carrying at shotgun. In the ensuing struggle, a shot was fired, blasting a hole in the ceiling, whereupon the gunman fled, leaving Richardson shaken but unharmed. Neilson's next victim would not be so lucky.

On February 15, 1974, Neilson broke into a post office in Harrogate, North Yorkshire and shot to death Donald Skepper, after the postmaster confronted him. Seven months later, he shot and killed Derek Astin, in almost identical circumstances during a robbery at Higher Baxenden, Lancashire. On November 11, Sidney Grayland, 55, was shot and killed at his post office in Oldbury, West Midlands, during a robbery that netted Neilson £800.

The police had by now linked the three murders, and the press had given the masked gunman the terrifying epithet, "The Black Panther."

However, the crime spree was not yet the media sensation that it would become. Neither were the takings anywhere near what Neilson was hoping for. It was time for a new plan, and one occurred to him while reading a story in the Daily Express in May 1972.

The article was about a 17-year-old heiress named Lesley Whittle, who'd just inherited £82, 500 (around half-a-million at current values) from her father's estate. Neilson had recently read an account of a kidnapping for ransom in the United States, where another young heiress had been held in an underground cell. He decided then and there to kidnap Lesley.

On the night of January 14, 1975, Neilson broke into the Whittle home in Highley, Shropshire and abducted Lesley from her bed, leaving behind a ransom demand for £50,000. He then drove the girl to Bathpool Park, near Kidsgrove, Staffordshire, where he left her, tethered by the neck, in a drainage shaft.

The following morning, Lesley's family found her bed empty and discovered the ransom demand. Neilson instructed Lesley's older brother, Ronald, to take £50,000 in used, low denomination banknotes to a telephone booth in Kidderminster, Worcestershire. He said that Lesley would be killed if the family contacted the police. Despite these instructions, the Whittle family immediately called in the local constabulary.

The police officer in charge of the investigation, Detective Chief Superintendent Bob Booth, assured the family that they'd done the right thing and promised to take every measure to ensure that the kidnapper was not alerted to police involvement. However, within hours, the story had leaked to the media and was receiving blanket coverage in the press and on radio and television. Booth then made another fatal mistake, instructing Ronald Whittle not to make the ransom drop. When the phone rang in the Kidderminster phone booth at midnight, no one was there to answer it.

A second ransom drop was planned for the following evening but had to be aborted when the press again got wind of it. Another 24 hours passed before the kidnapper called the Whittles' home and played a tape-recorded message by Lesley, giving instructions for another ransom drop, this time in Kidsgrove. This time, however,

Ronald Whittle was delayed by heavy traffic on the way to the drop site, arriving 90 minutes late. He was supposed to wait for a flashing light, signaling the drop, but the signal never came.

In the days that followed, the Whittle family waited anxiously for word from the kidnapper. Then, on January 22, 1975, Chief Superintendent Booth received a call from West Midlands Police about a seemingly unrelated crime. A security guard named Gerald Smith had been shot eight times in the back by an intruder at a rail terminal in Dudley. An abandoned car had been found nearby. Inside was a cassette tape with a recording of Lesley's voice, as well as four envelopes containing instructions for a new ransom drop.

Not long after, ballistics evidence from the Gerald Smith shooting linked the crime to the "Black Panther" murders. If the police had ever doubted it, they now knew that Lesley was in grave danger.

Chief Superintendent Booth immediately ordered a search of Bathpool Park, where the police soon discovered the drainage ditch. In it they found Lesley Whittle's emaciated corpse, hanging by the neck. It appeared that she'd either been pushed or had fallen from the ledge and had then strangled to death.

But the discovery of Lesley's body provided few clues as to the Black Panther's identity. In fact, had Donald Neilson decided to end his criminal career right there, he would likely have gotten away with murder. He didn't, though. He went back to robbing post offices.

On December 11, 1975, police constables Stuart McKenzie and Tony White were sitting in a police car in Mansfield, Nottinghamshire, when they spotted a man behaving furtively outside a post office. They called him over and asked him some routine questions, which the man answered. Then, without warning, he produced a shotgun from his bag and ordered them to drive him to Blidworth, some six miles away.

On route to that destination, PC White managed to distract Neilson and made a grab for the gun. McKenzie, meanwhile, stood on the brakes and slammed into the curb, in an effort to throw Neilson off balance. A vicious struggle ensued during which Neilson got out of the vehicle and fought for his life. It eventually took two passersby to help the police in subduing him.

A search of Neilson's home subsequently produced evidence that tied him to the Black Panther murders. He, however, continued to maintain his innocence for eight days, before he eventually cracked and admitted to the murders.

Tried at Oxford Crown Court in July 1976, he was given five life sentences with the stipulation that he must never be released.

# John Reginald Christie

*The Strangler of Rillington Place*

Number 10 Rillington Place was a grimy three-story terraced house in London's Notting Hill. The small Victorian building stood at the very end of a cul-de-sac bordering a factory wall. Nearby industrial plants belched smoke into the air and deposited grit on windowsills that were rattled night and day by passing trains.

These less than salubrious premises had been divided into three small flats, one occupying each floor. An outhouse in the garden served all three flats. There was no bathroom in the building, although there was a common washhouse.

John Reginald Christie and his wife Ethel moved into the ground floor flat at 10 Rillington Place in 1938, their lease incorporating exclusive use of the back garden. Christie was 40 at the time, a quiet, inconspicuous man, bald with an enormous forehead and watery, pale blue eyes behind thick spectacles. His wife was plump, big-boned and submissive. They seemed, to most outsiders, a quiet, pleasant couple, who were devoted to each other.

Christie was born in Halifax, Yorkshire on April 8, 1899. His father was a severe man who thought nothing of whipping the boy for the slightest infraction. Reg (as he was known) was a frail, sensitive child, coddled by his overprotective mother and dominated by his four older sisters.

As a child, he had few friends, although he did participate in sports and boy scouts. When Christie was eight, his paternal grandfather died and he was allowed to view the body, an experience that seemed to affect him profoundly.

Leaving school at the age of fifteen, he got a job as a projectionist in a movie theater. Then World War I arrived and was drafted, becoming a signalman. He only saw action once during his service, a mustard gas attack that left him temporarily blinded. He also lost his voice and remained without the power of speech for three years. Doctors who examined Christie determined that this was a hysterical reaction rather than due to physical damage. This would prove a lifelong pattern for Christie, who often feigned or exaggerated illness to avoid difficult situations.

After his discharge from the army, Christie got a job as a clerk. In 1920, he married Ethel Simpson Waddington, despite being mostly speechless during the courtship. The marriage remained unconsummated for over two years due to Christie's inability to perform with his wife. He did, however, frequent prostitutes during this time, something he'd done since the age of 19.

Early in the marriage, Christie became a postman, but he was fired after being caught stealing postal orders. He was sentenced to three months in prison. Upon his release, he abandoned Ethel in Sheffield and absconded to London. Christie held a series of short-term jobs over the next four years, before finding himself sentenced to a prison term of nine months, again for theft. After being released from that stint, he lived for a time with a prostitute but was again in trouble after he attacked the woman with a cricket bat. Another spell of incarceration followed a few years later, for stealing a car.

Christie had by this time been separated from his wife for almost ten years, but after his release he contacted Ethel and asked for a reconciliation. Lonely and starved for attention, Ethel agreed and joined Christie in London in 1933.

Not long after the reunion, Christie was hit by a car and had to be hospitalized. This only exacerbated his hypochondria. He regularly stayed off work and over the next 15 years would pay almost 200 visits to various doctors.

World War II was a godsend for Christie. Despite his lengthy criminal record, he volunteered for the War Reserve Police and was accepted. Over the next four years, he served as a Special Constable at Harrow Road Police Station, something he enjoyed immensely. Dressed in his uniform, pumped up on his own self-importance, he became fanatical about upholding the law, spying on and reporting his neighbors for the slightest infraction, an attitude which earned him the nickname, 'Himmler of Rillington Place.'

Not that Christie was above breaking the law himself. During Ethel's frequent visits to her relatives in Yorkshire, he continued to visit prostitutes. He also started a relationship with a woman who worked at the police station. When the woman's husband returned unexpectedly from the war, he found Christie in his house and beat him senseless. Thereafter, Christie began using his own home for his illicit trysts.

In the spring of 1948, ten years after the Christies had first moved to Rillington Place, Timothy Evans and his wife, Beryl, moved into the top flat. Beryl was 19, petite and pretty. Her husband was 24, an illiterate van driver from Merthyr Vale in Wales. The couple had been married less than a year and were expecting their first child. But already there were problems in the marriage. Beryl was obsessively jealous of her husband and often accused him of seeing other women. Timothy, for his part, was a habitual liar, prone to making up elaborate fantasies. Standing just five-foot-five and with an IQ that marked him as borderline retarded, he was a heavy drinker with a violent temper. The couple fought often, sometimes physically.

The arrival of the baby, Geraldine, hardly helped matters. Timothy's meager wages hardly covered the bills as it was, and the extra expense put an additional strain on the marriage. Then, to her horror, Beryl discovered that she was pregnant again.

Quite obviously, the young couple could not afford another child and Beryl decided early in the pregnancy to seek an abortion. It was just the opportunity Christie had been waiting for. He'd been lusting over the pretty young woman ever since she'd moved into the building, now he saw his chance.

Knowing that Beryl had already tried and failed to end her pregnancy with various pills, he offered to perform an abortion. Beryl was at first concerned but Christie stilled her fears, insisting that he'd done this many times before and had experience on medical matters due to his service in the police and military. Gullible and desperate, Beryl eventually agreed. Arrangements were made, with the procedure to be performed on November 8, while Ethel was out and Timothy Evans was at work. Christie and Beryl were not alone in the house though, there were workers on site repairing the roof and floorboards.

Only one person knows what happened next. According to Christie, he went in to see Beryl at around noon. She had already unfolded a quilt in front of the fire and laid it out in preparation. He tried to render her unconscious with gas but she panicked and he began hitting her. Then he got a cord and strangled her. He then tried to have sex with her, but couldn't (In another version, he says that he did penetrate her and the autopsy supports this).

When Evans came home that evening, Christie met him at the bottom of the stairs. He then followed Evans up to his flat. Once inside, Christie told Evans, "It's bad news. It didn't work." Christie pointed to the bedroom, where Beryl lay on the bed, covered up. When Evans pulled the blanket away, he saw that his wife was dead, with blood on her mouth, nose, and vagina.

Christie said that he thought Beryl had died from all the miscarriage remedies she had tried, but that both he and Evans would be in serious trouble if Evans went to the police. He then proposed that he would dispose of the body himself. Evans, in a state of panic and easily persuaded by the smooth-talking Christie, agreed. He helped Christie carry Beryl's body into the empty second floor flat, whose resident, Mr. Kitchener, was currently in hospital. Christie said he'd put the body down the drain outside after nightfall.

Evans then wanted to take the baby to his mother's house, but Christie dissuaded him, saying it would cause suspicion. He said he'd sleep on it and come up with a plan. The two then parted company.

The next morning, Christie told Evans that he knew a young couple who would take care of the baby. Christie said the couple would come the next day to collect her. That was the last day that anyone saw Geraldine alive.

Ludovic Kennedy who wrote the definitive book on the case, "Ten Rillington Place," believes that Christie strangled the little girl that day and placed her body with that of her mother. When the workmen were finished with their renovations, he carried the corpses down to the washhouse and hid them there. Christie then persuaded Evans to sell his furniture and leave town. Evans complied, fleeing back to Merthyr Vale.

Evans returned to London on November 23 and asked about his daughter. Christie told him that he could see her in two to three weeks but should lay low for now or he'd get them both into trouble. Evans then returned to his aunt's home in Wales where he told several untruths about Beryl's whereabouts. His aunt, Mrs. Probert, suspected that he was lying and she eventually challenged him on it. Not long after, she escorted him to Merthyr Tydfil police station, where he made the odd statement, "I have disposed of my wife. I put her down the drain."

He went on to tell a strange tale about meeting a man who'd given him something to abort Beryl's baby. Beryl had taken the pill but it had killed her. He had then taken the body and hidden it in the drain outside the front door. He made no mention of Christie.

The police in Wales weren't sure what to make of Evans' confession. Nonetheless, they made a call to the Notting Hill Police Station and arranged for officers to check out the story. The minute they tried to lift the manhole cover, they knew Evan's was lying. Three burly officers struggled to lift the heavy lid. There was no way Evans could have done it alone.

Back at Merthyr Vale, Evans was told that no body had been found. He seemed surprised but immediately changed his story, telling the truth this time. His neighbor, Reg Christie, had given Beryl the abortion pill, he said. He'd arrived home to find Beryl dead. He hadn't said this before, Evans explained, because Christie was an ex-police officer and he'd been afraid the police wouldn't believe him.

The police now returned to 10 Rillington Place and carried out a search, although this was superficial (they failed, for example, to notice the human thighbone being used to prop up a fence in the garden). What they did find, was a stolen briefcase in Evans' apartment.

Evans was arrested for theft and brought back to London for questioning. Christie was also questioned, as was Mrs. Christie, who told of Timothy's compulsive lying and his violent marriage to Beryl. Whether or not it was due to these revelations, the police decided to carry out another search. This time, they entered the washhouse where they discovered the bodies of Beryl and Geraldine Evans, hidden behind a pile of wood. Evans was charged with murder that same night and soon confessed to killing his wife and child.

Yet by the time the matter came to trial on January 11, 1950, Evans had withdrawn his confession, saying it had been coerced from him under threat of physical violence. There are a number of compelling reasons to believe that this might have been the case. Most compelling is a key inaccuracy in the statement - Evans could not have concealed the bodies behind the pile of wood where they were found because on the day he claimed to have done so, the boards had not yet been placed there by the workers.

Nonetheless, this key piece of information, along with others, never reached the ears of the jury. What they did hear was a damning account by the key prosecution witness, John Reginald Christie. Evans was found guilty. On March 9, 1950, he went to the gallows, still protesting his innocence.

Following the trial, Christie went into a deep depression, losing 28 pounds. His hypochondria got worse. He visited the doctor 33 times in eight months and was eventually hospitalized for three weeks. During this time, he also lost his job due to disclosures at the trial about his criminal past. He got another job, but quit soon after, saying he could do better.

Ethel, too, was unhappy, not just because Christie was unemployed, but because Mr. Kitchener had moved out and been replaced by a family of Jamaicans who frightened her. She wanted to leave Rillington Place, but with Christie unemployed, they were unable to do so.

On Thursday, December 11, five days after Christie had quit his job, Ethel went to watch television with a friend, Rosie. The next day, she was seen at a local laundry and seemed well and cheerful. It was the last time she was seen alive.

On Monday, Christie posted a letter that Ethel had earlier written to her sister in Sheffield, changing the date to make it appear as though she'd written it later.

Then, he began to tell neighbors that his wife had gone to Sheffield and that he'd soon be moving there himself. To Ethel's relatives, he said that Ethel was not feeling well enough to write to them. He did, however, send Christmas cards and a few gifts signed "from Ethel and Reg."

In January, Christie sold all of his furniture to a dealer and continued living in the near empty flat, sleeping on an old mattress on the floor. He also sold his wife's wedding band and watch. By

March, he had emptied Ethel's bank account and was no longer bothering to respond to her relatives' enquiries about her whereabouts.

On March 19, he met a woman, Mrs. Reilly, who was looking for a place to rent. Christie offered her and her husband his flat, claiming he owned it. The Reilly's decided to take the flat for which Christie demanded three months rent in advance. He moved out the next day.

The Reillys were only in the flat for one day before the real landlord arrived and told them that Christie had had no right to let the premises to them. He asked them to leave and, with the premises now empty, gave permission for the upstairs tenant, Beresford Brown, to use the kitchen. Brown decided that the place could use a clean up and in the process of doing so decided to screw an eyehook into the wall for him to hang his radio from. He began to knock on the surface, trying to find a spot and it was then that he realized that part of the wall sounded hollow. Assuming that there was a cupboard behind it, he started peeling back the wallpaper.

With a few strips of paper removed, Brown noticed a gap in the plasterboard and shone a light through it. He pulled back instantly, shocked by what he thought he'd just seen. He was certain that there was a naked woman in there.

Brown contacted the police who were soon on the scene. Yet when they opened the door they were shocked to find, not one corpse, but three. An autopsy would later reveal that all three had been strangled. The bodies were remarkably well preserved and also showed signs of gas asphyxiation. Neither was this the last surprise awaiting the police – under some loose flooring, they found a fourth female corpse, also strangled.

The fourth victim was quickly identified as Ethel Christie and an identification of the other three soon followed. All three were prostitutes; Hectorina McLennan, 26; Kathleen Maloney, 26; and Rita Nelson, 25. All had died within the last 12-15 weeks.

Going through the rest of the flat, the police found a man's tie fashioned into a reef knot, a quantity of potassium cyanide and a tobacco tin containing four clumps of pubic hair - none of which matched the victims in the kitchen.

The police also searched the garden and, this time, they noticed the human femur. There were also bones in the flowerbeds as well as blackened skull fragments and a number of teeth. Although, only one skull was recovered the pathologist determined that two bodies had been buried in the garden, both of them female.

The first victim was 21-year-old Ruth Margarete Fuerst, an Austrian national who'd been missing since August 24, 1943. The second was likely to be Muriel Amelia Eady, 32, who had worked at a factory with Christie at the time of her disappearance. That made six bodies discovered at 10 Rillington Place. Now the search was on to find the likely killer.

After leaving Rillington Place, Christie placed his suitcase into a locker and began wandering aimlessly around London. On March

20, 1953, he booked a room at a King's Cross boarding house using his real name and address. He paid for seven nights, but left after four, by which time his name and face were plastered on the front page of every newspaper.

As his money began to run out, Christie took to sleeping on park benches and in movies theaters. Eventually, he took to wandering along the banks of the Thames and it was there that he was arrested near Putney Bridge on March 31. He'd been on the loose for ten days.

At Putney Police station, Christie willingly confessed to four murders and hinted that there was something else that he could not quite remember, an obvious ploy to try and find out if the police had discovered the skeletons in the garden.

Christie had a ready excuse for each of the murders. Of his wife, he said that he'd woken up to find her blue in the face and choking. He tried to resuscitate her, but unable to do so he decided to end her suffering by strangling her. He'd later found an empty pill bottle and assumed that Ethel had tried to kill herself.

The other three women were also "not his fault." He said he'd met Rita Nelson on the street on January 19, 1953. She allegedly demanded money from him, saying she'd scream and accuse him of attacking her if he didn't give her 30 shillings. He walked away but she followed him back to his house, forcing her way in. She then picked up a frying pan and tried to hit him. They struggled and she fell back on a chair that had a rope hanging from it. Christie blacked out and woke up to find her dead.

In February, he met Kathleen Maloney, 26, in a Notting Hill café. Learning that she was searching for a flat, he offered to help. Kathleen went home with Christie but once there she threatened violence if he didn't use his influence with the landlord to get her a flat. He blacked out and when he revived she was dead. He did not remember killing her.

Of Hectorina McLennan, Christie said that he gave her and her boyfriend a place to stay. However, after a few days, he asked them to leave. Hectorina later returned alone. Christie tried to get her to leave and they struggled. After a while, she went limp and sank to the floor. Christie believed that some of her clothing may have got wrapped around her neck and choked her.

He later told a different version of events, one that rings truer. He said he invited Hectorina to his house for a drink. Once there he got her to sit in a chair over which he'd constructed a special canopy. He then turned on the gas. Hectorina tried to leave but he caught her at the door and throttled her into unconsciousness. He'd then had sex with her before finishing her off with the gas.

Confronted with evidence regarding the murders of Ruth Fuerst, and Muriel Eady, he readily admitted to killing them, although he denied murdering Beryl Evans and her daughter. Later, he admitted to killing Beryl but denied killing Geraldine. (Ludovic Kennedy firmly believes that Christie did kill the baby, but that the act was so traumatic to him that he wiped it from his memory.)

Christie was held at Brixton prison, pending his trial. He was examined by several psychiatrists, who registered a universal dislike for the man, describing him as "nauseating" and "sniveling." He had a habit of dropping his voice to a whisper whenever he was asked a question that he did not like. He also spoke of himself in the third person as though dissociating himself from his deeds.

With the other inmates, though, it was a different story. Christie boasted about his deeds, comparing himself to the infamous acid bath killer, John George Haigh, murderer of six people. Christie said that he had planned on outdoing Haigh by killing 12.

John Reginald Christie went on trial at the Old Bailey on June 22nd, 1953. His defense pleaded him Not Guilty by Reason of Insanity and produced expert witnesses to testify as to the veracity of this. The prosecution produced their own witnesses to testify that Christie was sane and therefore guilty.

The trial lasted only four days, and the jury deliberated for only an hour and 20 minutes before pronouncing Christie guilty. He was sentenced to death.

Christie did not appeal and went to the gallows at Pentonville Prison on July 15, 1953.

Yet that was not the end of the case. In the wake of Christie's trial many now believed that the state had hanged an innocent man in Timothy Evans. An inquiry was hastily convened and after just 11 days concluded that Evans had indeed strangled his wife and baby.

However, this verdict was unsatisfactory to many observers. Two years later, a delegation of four press editors approached the Home Secretary to request another inquiry. Their request was denied, as was a subsequent application.

Eventually, in 1965, a new inquiry was conducted. It reached a strange conclusion, deciding that Evans had strangled his wife but not his daughter. As Evans had been tried only for the murder of his daughter, High Court Judge, Sir Daniel Brabin, granted him a posthumous pardon in 1966. This did not declare him innocent, only innocent of the charge for which he was tried – the murder of his daughter.

The evidence, however, suggests that Christie killed, both Beryl and Geraldine, as well as the six other women found concealed at 10 Rillington Place.

# John Duffy and David Mulcahy

*The Railway Killers*

*"We did it as a bit of a joke, a bit of a game." – John Duffy*

The science of a criminal profiling is an important investigative tool these days, a cornerstone of any serial homicide investigation. However, there was a time when such techniques were ridiculed by law enforcement officers, considered about as useful as phrenology or palm reading. The case that changed all that was the pursuit of the so-called, 'Railway Killer,' a brutal serial killer who raped and murdered three women in London during the mid-1980's.

The murders were, in fact, the culmination of a protracted crime spree. Beginning in 1982, a series of violent rapes had been committed in and around train stations across London, Surrey, and the Home Counties. The perpetrators were two masked men, working together. Over the next 12 months, 18 women would fall prey to this sinister duo, described by their victims as working with an almost telepathic understanding of each other.

Then, in 1983 the attacks mysteriously ceased, only to resume again in 1984. This time, though, the perpetrator was a sole rapist and his attacks were far more frequent, culminating in 1985 with three rapes in a single night.

Something clearly had to be done to stop this criminal and the police responded by launching Operation Hart, one of Britain's biggest criminal investigations ever. Yet, despite the breadth of this undertaking the police had very little to go on. They had figured out by now that the rapist had an in-depth knowledge of the rail system and they knew that the man they sought was small in stature. Other than that, the only description they had was of the criminal's eyes, said to be, "cold blue, staring, almost like lasers."

They knew also that he carried a knife and must have feared that, unless they caught him soon, someone was going to get seriously hurt.

On the cold afternoon of December 29, 1985, 19-year-old Alison Day left her home in Hornchurch, Essex and boarded a bus for Hackney Wick railway station. Her fiancé, Paul Tidiman, was working overtime that day, and the pair had agreed to meet up at the printing works where Paul was employed. This was just a short walk from the station, but in order to reach it, Alison had to walk down a darkened path that ran alongside a canal. It was on that path that she met her killer.

When Alison didn't show, Paul became anxious. Eventually, he left work and walked to the nearby station where he stood on the platform, calling her name. Little did he know that she lay just 100 yards away, raped and murdered.

A massive search was launched but turned up nothing until January 15, 1986, when Allison's body was found floating face down in the River Lee. Her blouse had been cut into three pieces, two of which had been used to gag and bind her.

The third piece was round her neck, used as a tourniquet to strangle her. The killer had placed stones in the pocket of her sheepskin coat in an effort to sink the body. Two weeks in the water had unfortunately obliterated any forensic evidence, but there were fibers on the coat, which the police believed must have come from the killer.

The officers investigating Alison's murder shared their findings with the Operation Hart team, but apart from the obvious railway connection, there was nothing to link the two cases. The Hart investigators did not believe that their man was responsible.

It was a tragic mistake. Four months later, the killer struck again.

Maartje Tamboezer was just 15-years-old, one of 3 sisters, the daughter of a Dutch businessman living in West Horsley, Surrey. On the afternoon of Thursday, April 17, 1986, Maartje was excited about her upcoming holiday. She wanted to buy some candy to take with her on the trip and in late afternoon, she decided to cycle to the nearby village of East Horsley. When she hadn't returned by early evening, her frantic parents called the Surrey Police.

The next morning, two men walking along a path that ran adjacent to the A246, between Guildford and Leatherhead came across Maartje's body. She was bound by the wrists and had been savagely beaten. The tourniquet that had strangled her was still around her neck and the killer had tried to set fire to her corpse, presumably in an effort to obliterate forensic evidence. Her bicycle was found nearby, propped against a tree.

The police also came across an interesting clue, a length of bright orange rope stretched across the footpath at chest height. This had obviously been set there in order to force a cyclist coming up the path to stop and dismount. Detectives surmised that Maartje had then been dragged into nearby woods, raped, beaten, and finally garroted. Aside from the rope, police found an unusually small footprint at the scene, and the post-mortem yielded another clue. One of the victim's neck bones was broken, and the pathologist believed that the injury had been caused by a 'karate blow.'

As Surrey police continued their enquiries, they got their most promising lead yet. Passengers traveling on the 6:07 pm train from Horsley to London, on the day of the murder, reported a man rushing onto the platform as the train was departing, and trying to force his way onto the train, resulting in the guard having to reopen the self-closing doors. The man was small in stature and more than one passenger described him as having piercing blue eyes. The police wondered whether this might not be the man who had left the footprint at the crime scene. They checked thousands of discarded train tickets for fingerprints but came up empty.

There were, however, additional clues from the crime scene. Semen lifted from the victim gave the killer's blood type as group A. Then there was the string used to bind the girl's hands. It was from a brand called Somyarn and was unusual in that it was made from paper, not the normal hessian or plastic.

The police were still following up on these leads when the Railway Killer struck again. The victim was a 29-year-old secretary named Anne Lock. Anne had recently married and had only just returned from her honeymoon in the Seychelles. On the night of Sunday, May 18, she worked late at her job at London Weekend Television. After finishing her shift, she took a train to Brookman's Park near Potter's Bar, Hertfordshire, arriving there at around 10 p.m. Alighting the train, she walked quickly towards the bicycle shed where she had left her bike. She was never seen alive again.

The disappearance of Anne Lock was soon linked to the murders of Alison Day and Maartje Tamboezer, and resulted in Surrey and Hertfordshire police working together to launch the biggest manhunt undertaken in Britain since the Yorkshire Ripper inquiry of the 1970's. Information on the murders was also fed into the Operation Hart database, enabling detectives to narrow their initial list of over 5000 suspects down to 1,999. Number 1,594 on the list was John Duffy, a slightly built Irishman, who worked as a carpenter for British Rail.

Duffy had earned himself a place on the list due to a charge that he raped his (then estranged, now ex) wife in August 1985. Then, on Saturday, May 17, 1986, he was arrested for loitering at North Weald Railway station and found to be in possession of a butterfly knife. Duffy said that the knife was for use in his martial arts class, and without evidence of any offense, the police had no option but to release him. However, details of his arrest were logged with the police and on July 17, he was brought in for questioning.

He arrived with a solicitor in tow and refused to give a blood sample, immediately arousing suspicion. Detectives also couldn't help but notice that he fit the description of the man they sought, small of stature, with pockmarked skin, and those piercing blue eyes that several victims had described. His reference to a martial arts class also got detectives thinking about the broken bone in Maartje Tamboezer's neck, and how the pathologist believed a karate blow might have caused it.

Four days later, a maintenance team discovered Anne Lock's body on an overgrown embankment near Brookmans Park Station. Like the other victims she had been garroted, her hands bound with the same coarse string. The killer had also tried to burn her body.

With the discovery of Anne Lock's body, detectives decided to bring Duffy in for a second round of questioning. To their astonishment, they found that he had been admitted to a psychiatric hospital in North London and that doctors there refused to allow him to be questioned. Duffy claimed that he had been attacked by two men and had lost his memory as a result. The police were skeptical about his claims but couldn't disprove them. Duffy would remain at the hospital for a month, while the police moved on to other suspects.

He was at liberty again by the time a 14-year-old Watford schoolgirl was raped on October 21. The girl described her attacker as small, with a pockmarked face and piercing blue eyes. She also said that he had a German Shepherd Dog with him, who he referred to as Bruce.

The description was a close match for Duffy, and he was rapidly elevated to the top of the suspect list and placed under surveillance. The police were by now almost certain that Duffy was their man. Yet they lacked any concrete evidence against him. In order to firm up their case, they turned to an unusual source.

Criminal profiling had already been in use in the United States for a decade, with experts like John Douglas and Robert Ressler, of the FBI's Behavioral Sciences unit, at the forefront of the technology. However, it was still in its infancy in Britain, so when the task force decided to develop a profile for the Railway Killer, the looked to Professor David Canter, a professor of Applied Psychology at the University of Surrey.

Canter was an expert in Behavioral Science, but he had never worked with the police before. When asked to develop the profile, he spent two weeks reading over witness statements and forensic reports as well as mapping the sites of each of the attacks. Eventually, he produced his report, presenting the police with 17 points about the character and behavior of the killer. He even made a prediction as where the killer lived.

Professor Canter's profile would prove to be remarkably accurate, with 13 out of his 17 indicators matching the killer, including; the area where he lived, his marital status, his age, build, occupation, and interests. When the police fed this information into the database and compared it against their suspect list, only one name was returned – John Duffy.

On Sunday 23 November 1986, senior detectives ordered Duffy's arrest and a search of his home. This turned up a wealth of incriminating evidence, including a ball of Somyarn string and fibers similar to those found on Alison Day's body. Both would be forensically matched to the victims. The also discovered that Duffy had a German Shepherd Dog named Bruce, as mentioned by one of his victims.

Duffy's trial was held at London's Old Bailey, 14 months later. Many of his rape victims could not bring themselves to face him in court, but five of them did give evidence. He entered not guilty pleas on all charges but was eventually found guilty on five counts of rape and two of murder. In the case of Anne Lock, the jury returned an acquittal due to lack of evidence. He displayed no emotion as he was handed 8 life sentences.

Despite his conviction, Duffy refused to name his accomplice, the man who had committed at least 16 rapes with him and who police believed was also involved in the murders.

They suspected David Mulcahy, a lifelong friend of Duffy, but despite six days of questioning and numerous searches of his home, the Operation Hart team failed to turn up any evidence. Emboldened by this, Mulcahy had arrogantly mocked the police when Duffy was jailed, even threatening to sue for wrongful arrest.

Ten years passed and, with Duffy safely behind bars, and maintaining his silence, Mulcahy must have believed he had gotten away with murder. But then, on August 6, 1996, another rapist began operating on Hampstead Heath, setting off a chain of events that would eventually bring David Mulcahy to justice.

The rapist's name was Ted Biggs, and he would rape six women before a police operation, dubbed Operation Loudwater, eventually snared him. Before that happened, one of the Loudwater team, DC Caroline Murphy, met DC John Haye in a pub. Haye had worked on the Duffy investigation.

The two got talking and quickly realized the similarities between the two cases.

The next day, DC Murphy called Whitehouse prison to ascertain that Duffy was still behind bars, and could not be responsible for offenses she was investigating. During the course of that inquiry, Murphy learned that Duffy had given the name of his accomplice as David Mulcahy.

At the time of Duffy and Mulcahy's murderous spree, DNA profiling was not available. Now, though, the surviving evidence was re-examined and turned up a match to Mulcahy. Police also found a blunder made by the original investigative team, a fingerprint belonging to David Mulcahy on a rope that had been used to bind one of the victims.

Mulcahy was arrested and with the DNA evidence against him, prosecutors were confident of a conviction. That conviction became a forgone conclusion when John Duffy agreed to testify, revealing details about the murders that had never been heard before.

Duffy and Mulcahy had known each other all their lives. They made an odd pair, the towering, powerfully-build Mulcahy and the diminutive, pockmarked Duffy. Yet they had been almost inseparable, drawn to each other by a shared love for martial arts and a mutual appetite for cruelty. As youngsters, they got their kicks scaring homosexuals and courting couples on Hampstead Heath, and indulging in acts of animal cruelty.

Then, in 1976 they were convicted of causing actual bodily harm after they shot four victims with an air rifle. Shortly afterward, Mulcahy suggested for the first time that they should rape a woman together.

It is easy to see how such an idea would have appeal to the monstrous pair. Each man was plagued by deep feelings of sexual inadequacy - Duffy's due to a low sperm count, which prevented him from fathering children; Mulcahy through difficulties in maintaining an erection during normal sex.

According to Duffy, their first victim was meant to be a woman from Hendon, north London, who Mulcahy wanted to 'teach her a lesson.' They broke into the woman's house but left when she failed to come home. Another planned rape was foiled when the woman returned home with a male friend.

In 1981, the pair found themselves in court on a theft charge, but escaped with suspended sentences. A year later, they launched the horrific series of rapes that would culminate in murder.

Duffy and Mulcahy became quite accomplished at their craft. They'd prepare a 'rapist's kit,' consisting of balaclavas, knives and tape to gag and blindfold their victims. Then they'd hit the streets, cruising and singing along to the sounds of Michael Jackson's 'Thriller.'

As time went by, Mulcahy began to become more and more sadistic. He'd taunt his victims, threatening to gouge their eyes out or slice off their nipples. Their terror seemed to turn him on. He became more physically violent too. On one occasion, Duffy described having to break off an attack because he feared Mulcahy would kill the 16-year-old victim. A month later, according to Duffy, he stopped another attack because of Mulcahy' rage. It was clear by now that the sexual thrill was not enough for Mulcahy. He wanted more.

Four days after Christmas 1985, they targeted Alison Day, forcing her from a path near Hackney Wick station and dragging her to some snow covered playing fields nearby. After both men had raped Alison, she tried to escape and fell into the freezing water of a feeder canal. Duffy claimed he pulled her out, but Mulcahy was so excited by the incident that he raped the terrified girl again. He then tore off a piece of Alison's blouse and started strangling her.

As the girl begged for her life Mulcahy twisted the blouse into a tourniquet and strangled her. Later, he told Duffy: "It is God-like - having the decision over life and death."

On April 17, 1986, the pair laid a trap by tying a length of rope across a bicycle path. When 15-year-old Maartje Tamboezer stopped her bike to go around it, they grabbed her and dragged her into some woods where both men raped her.

Mulcahy then struck the girl with a rock to the side of the head, knocking her unconscious. Then, he took Maartje's belt and looped it around her throat, before slotting a stick under the belt to form a garrotte. He allegedly told Duffy: "I did the last one, you'll do this one."

After Maartje was dead, they both left the scene, but Mulcahy returned later and set the body alight, stuffing burning tissues into her vagina hoping to destroy forensic evidence.

Just over a month later, the pair ambushed Anne Lock at Brookmans Park station in Hertfordshire on May 18, 1986. According to Duffy, he raped Anne. Then, Mulcahy threw him a bunch of keys and told him to fetch the car. When he returned, Mulcahy told him: "I've taken care of it. She won't identify us now." Duffy said that Mulcahy was buzzing on the drive home. He kept saying: "Keep your eyes open for another one."

Mulcahy was convicted of three murders, seven rapes and five charges of conspiracy to rape. He was sentenced to several life terms. Neither he nor Duffy will ever be released.

# Peter Tobin

Peter Britton Tobin was born on August 27, 1946, in Johnstone, Renfrewshire, the youngest of seven children. He showed early signs of aberrant behavior and at the age of just seven he was sent to a special school for difficult children. Not that the school did much to change his conduct, he'd barely been released when he was arrested on charges of burglary and sent to a juvenile institution. He'd serve numerous terms in reformatories, eventually graduating to an adult prison in 1970, when he was convicted on charges of burglary and forgery.

Tobin was by then living in England, having moved to Brighton in 1969. He was also married, but Margaret Mountney divorced him in 1971, citing spousal abuse. He'd marry twice more, and father three children. However, each of these marriages would end in divorce, the women always telling a similar story. Tobin would start out charming and attentive but soon turn to sadistic violence.

In August 1993, Tobin was living in the town of Havant, Hampshire. On August 4, he hired two 14-year old girls to babysit his son. He then forced the girls at knifepoint to drink vodka and cider before sexually assaulting and raping them.

Tobin warned the girls not to report the incident, but he took precautions anyway. By the time the police arrived to arrest him, he was long gone, fled to a religious retreat in nearby Warwickshire. He lived there for months under an assumed name but was identified after the BBC ran a segment about his case on its Crime Watch program.

Brought before Winchester Crown Court on May 18, 1994, Tobin pleaded guilty, and received a 14-year prison term. He served ten, and was released in 2004, whereupon he moved to Paisley, in his native Scotland. In May 2007, he was back in prison, serving 30 months for breaching the conditions of his parole.

Given the trajectory Peter Tobin's life was on, it seems inevitable that he'd eventually graduate to murder. In September 2006, he was working as a handyman at St. Patrick's Roman Catholic Church in Glasgow. Once again in contravention of his parole, he'd taken on an assumed name, "Pat McLaughlin."

At that time, a 23-year-old Polish student named Angelika Kluk was living at the chapel, working part-time as a cleaner in order to finance her studies. Kluk was last seen alive on September 24, 2006. Five days later, her brutalized body was discovered hidden under some floorboards in the church. She'd been beaten, raped, and stabbed to death. Forensic evidence would later suggest that she was still alive when her body was placed under the floor.

"Pat McLaughlin" meanwhile, was nowhere to be found. He'd fled to London and checked himself into a hospital under yet another alias. He was arrested there a few days later.

Peter Tobin went on trial at the Edinburgh High Court in March 2007. Found guilty of rape and murder, he was sentenced to life in prison, with the stipulation that he must serve at least 21 years before being eligible for parole.

However, the story of Peter Tobin doesn't end there. The police had long suspected him in the 1991 disappearance of a 15-year-old girl named Vicky Hamilton. Vicky was last seen on February 10, 1991, waiting for a bus in Bathgate, West Lothian. Tobin had been living in the town at the time, but true to his usual M.O., he'd moved away days after Vicky's disappearance.

In July 2007, the police carried out a search of Tobin's house and announced soon after that they'd charged a man in connection with Vicky Hamilton's death. In early October, they searched another of Tobin's former homes, in England, where he'd fled after leaving Bathgate.

On November 14, 2007, the police announced that remains found buried in the back garden of a house in Margate, Kent, were those of Vicky Hamilton. They also confirmed that the body of another young woman (later identified as Dinah McNicol) had also been discovered.

Tobin went on trial for Vicky Hamilton's murder in December 2008. Found guilty, he was sentenced to an additional life term.

On December 14, 2009, he was back in court, charged with the murder of Dinah McNicol. Dinah had last been seen alive on August 5, 1991, when she was hitchhiking home from a music festival in the company of a male companion. A driver had picked them up and later dropped the man off, while Vicky remained in the car. She was never seen alive again. In the days after her disappearance, regular withdrawals continued to be made from her bank account.

The jury took less than 15 minutes to convict Tobin of Dinah McNicol's murder. A third life term was tacked onto his sentence, with the judge recommending that Tobin never be released.

However, the three murders for which he has been convicted are unlikely to be the full extent of Tobin's killing spree. The police have since assembled a task force to investigate 13 more homicides in which his involvement is suspected, while Tobin privately boasts to his fellow inmates that he has committed 48 murders.

There is also evidence to suggest that Tobin might be Bible John, an as yet unidentified serial killer who terrorized Glasgow during the late sixties. Tobin was living in the area at the time that Bible John claimed his three victims, and a police sketch drawn up from eyewitness accounts bears a remarkable resemblance to him. Coincidentally, the Bible John killings ended after Tobin left Scotland in 1969.

# Amelia Dyer

## The Reading Baby Farmer

*"You'll know mine by the tape around their necks." - Amelia Dyer*

The advertisement in the classified pages of the Bristol Times was heartrending but sadly common in Victorian England. "Wanted," it read, "respectable woman to take young child."

The ad had been placed there by Evelina Marmon, a barmaid at the Plough Hotel in Cheltenham. Two months earlier, in January 1896, Evelina had given birth to a baby girl she named Doris. The child's father had since deserted her, leaving her with a daughter she loved but was unable to care for. She would have to have Doris "adopted out," in the parlance of the time, so that she could continue working and hopefully reclaim her child once her financial situation improved.

As chance would have it, the advertisement placed directly alongside her own seemed like the answer to her prayers. It read: "Married couple with no family would adopt healthy child, nice country home. Terms, £10." Evelina quickly wrote a response and posted it to the advertiser, a Mrs. Harding of Reading.

Before long, she had a response, one that eased her conscience somewhat. Mrs. Harding seemed like exactly the foster mother she wanted for young Doris. "I should be glad to have a dear little baby girl," she wrote. "One I could bring up and call my own. We are plain, homely people, in fairly good circumstances. I don't want a child for money's sake, but for company and home comfort. Myself and my husband are dearly fond of children. I have no child of my own. A child with me will have a good home and a mother's love."

Another round of letters followed in which Mrs. Harding stressed that she would be a devoted mother to the child, adding: "It is just lovely here, healthy and pleasant. There is an orchard opposite our front door." She also assured Evelina that she could visit whenever she pleased.

The only issue to be resolved was the matter of payment. Evelina, in her financially strapped situation, had hoped to pay a weekly fee for her daughter's upkeep. However, Mrs. Harding insisted on the full amount of £10 up front. Eventually, the desperate mother agreed, and a week later Mrs. Harding arrived in Cheltenham.

Evelina was expecting a young or middle-aged woman, so she was surprised by the elderly, heavy-set, Mrs. Harding. Nonetheless, the woman seemed affectionate enough, as she quickly wrapped little Doris in the warm shawl she'd brought with her. The transaction was completed when Evelina handed over a cardboard box of clothes and the agree-upon £10. In exchange, Mrs. Harding gave her a signed receipt.

Unable and unwilling to take leave of her daughter so easily, Evelina accompanied Mrs. Harding on the train as far as Gloucester. There she stood weeping on the platform as the 5.20 train took her daughter away from her. She returned to her home a forlorn, broken woman.

Unbeknownst to Evelina she had just fallen victim to one of the most evil schemes to plague Victorian England. The woman to whom she'd just entrusted her baby to was none other than Amelia Dyer, a heartless brute who was engaged in the vile practice of baby farming.

Amelia Dyer was born in the small village of Pyle Marsh, just east of Bristol. Her father, Samuel Hobley, was a master shoemaker and, unlike many of her generation, Amelia and her four older siblings grew up in fairly comfortable circumstances. All was not well in the family, though, Amelia's mother suffered from mental illness, caused by typhus. She died in 1848, with Amelia nursing her up to the time of her death.

After her mother's death, Amelia lived with an aunt in Bristol and served an apprenticeship with a corset maker. Her father died in 1859, and not long after, Amelia became estranged from her family. She moved into lodgings in Trinity Street, Bristol. There she met, and later married, George Thomas, 35 years her senior.

After a couple of years of marriage, Amelia decided to train as a nurse, a particularly grueling occupation in Victorian times, but one that was considered a respectable livelihood. It was during this time that she met Ellen Dane, a midwife who told her about the easy pickings to be made as a "baby farmer."

Unwed mothers were at a severe disadvantage in Victorian England. Not only were the fathers of illegitimate children absolved of any financial obligation for their upkeep, but illegitimacy carried with it a stigma. Single mothers were prevented from gaining employment, finding accommodation, even from being accepted into a workhouse.

This situation gave rise to an entire industry, a sub-culture of individuals who acted as adoption or fostering agents. In return for a single upfront payment, or a monthly fee, these "baby farmers," would (theoretically) take over responsibility for the infant's care.

I say, theoretically, because more often than not, the baby received little if any care, at all. Many unscrupulous "caregivers" resorted to starving the children in their custody, either to save money or to deliberately cause death. "Difficult" or noisy babies were simply kept sedated (a popular sedative of the era was Godfrey's Cordial - known colloquially as "Mother's Friend" or "The Quietness"). This easily obtained syrup contained opium and was used to lull children to sleep. Unfortunately, overuse (which was common) also suppressed the appetite, leading to death from malnutrition. A doctor would then record the cause of death as "debility from birth," or "lack of breast milk," and the baby farmer would pocket what remained of the adoption fee. Needless, to say the unscrupulous soon saw the money making potential in hastening the deaths of their young charges.

This was the scheme proposed to the Amelia Dyer by her new friend Ellen Danes (who was soon forced to flee the country with the authorities hot on her trail). Then, in 1869, George Thomas died, leaving Amelia with no income and an infant daughter to care for.

Amelia turned to providing lodging for expectant single mothers, but she soon realized the much better returns to be gained from baby farming. Soon she was running newspaper ads offering to adopt babies for a substantial one-off payment plus adequate clothing for the child. In her advertisements and subsequent meetings with potential clients, she assured them that she was respectable, married, and that she would provide a safe and loving home for the child.

However, this was wide of the truth. From her earliest days as a baby farmer, Dyer was neglecting the children in her care, allowing them to succumb to malnutrition. Eventually though, she decided that these methods took too much of her time and ate too deeply into her profits. It was then that she decided to simply murder the children soon after they were handed over to her. In this way, she was able to pocket the entire adoption fee.

However, even in 19th century England, when infant mortality was as high as one in two and child welfare a distant priority, Dyer's activities, drew attention. In 1879, a doctor became suspicious of the number of child deaths he had been called by Dyer to certify. He alerted the authorities and Dyer found herself under arrest. Instead of being tried for murder, though, the charge was neglect. Dyer got six months at hard labor, a ridiculously lenient sentence in an era when petty theft could result in transportation to the colonies.

After her release, Dyer attempted to resume her nursing career but she soon fell back into the murky world of baby farming. During this time, she had a number of spells in mental hospitals, allegedly due to her suicidal tendencies. However, it would later be caustically noted that these episodes always seemed to occur just when the police were closing in on her criminal enterprise. Dyer was all too adept at mimicking psychotic behavior, having nursed her mother through mental disease and having served as a nurse in a psychiatric ward. As soon as the heat was off, she always seemed to make a miraculous recovery.

In 1890, Dyer again came under suspicion from the authorities resulting in her suffering an apparent breakdown and trying to take her own life. She survived, and the experience did nothing to discourage her from her monstrous trade. In fact, all it did was to teach her the folly of involving doctors to issue death certificates. She'd also long since learned that in order to stay ahead of the authorities (and anxious mothers seeking to reclaim their children) she had to relocate frequently. Year on year, Dyer dodged the police and the inspectors of the newly formed NSPCC. She ran her baby farming operations from locations in Bristol, Reading, Cardiff, and London. She also used a number of aliases.

In 1893, Dyer was discharged from another committal at Wells mental asylum. Two years later, she moved to Caversham, Berkshire. By now, she had her 23-year-old daughter, Mary Ann (known as Polly) in tow, as well as Polly's husband, Arthur Palmer. She'd also acquired an associate, although Jane "Granny" Smith appears to have been oblivious to Dyer's criminal activities. Her primary activity seems to have been to pose as Dyer's mother when meeting with potential clients, in order to present the image of a happy, extended family.

In January 1896, Dyer took in Evelina Marmon's daughter, Doris. However, rather than take the baby to Reading, as she'd told Marmon, she went instead to 76 Mayo Road, Willesden, London where she was staying with her daughter. Once inside their rented rooms, Dyer rifled through a tangle of threads in a workbox and found some white edging tape, used in dressmaking. She wound the tape twice around Doris's neck, then pulled it tight, held it for a few seconds and tied it in a knot. Death would not have been instantaneous. Doris would have struggled for breath, her mouth opening and closing as she fought instinctively for life. Then her limbs would have gone limp as she asphyxiated. Dyer would later admit: "I used to like to watch them with the tape around their neck, but it was soon all over with them."

With the baby dead, the two women wrapped the tiny corpse in a napkin. They then went through the pitiful bundle of clothes Evelina had sent with her daughter, picking out the best items, setting the rest aside for the pawnbroker. With the £10, Dyer had taken from Evelina, she paid the rent and gave her unwitting landlady a pair of Doris's boots as a present for her little girl.

The very next day, April 1, 1896, another infant, 13-month-old Harry Simmons, was brought to Mayo Road in return for a £10 payment. Dyer searched around for another piece of tape to dispatch the infant. Finding none, she removed the tape from Doris's neck and used the same piece to strangle the little boy.

On the following evening, the two tiny corpses were stuffed into Dyer's carpetbag and weighted down with bricks. She then took the bus to Paddington and the train to Reading. There she hauled the heavy bag to a footbridge at Caversham Lock, an area she knew well. Under cover of darkness, she forced the bag through the railings and dropped it into the river. She walked away fully believing that the bodies would never be discovered.

Unbeknownst to Dyer, the net had already begun to close in on her. On 30 March 1896, a bargeman had retrieved a package from the Thames at Reading. He was shocked to find that it contained the body of a baby girl (later identified as Helena Fry). The police were called and the officer assigned to the case, Detective Constable Anderson, almost immediately found a crucial clue. Attached to the wrapping paper was a label with a barely discernible name, "Mrs. Thomas," and an address in Reading.

The police visited that address but found that Mrs. Thomas had already flown the coop. They were, however, able to track her to the house in Mayo Road, Willesden. Yet even though they'd found the suspect, the police had no evidence that she'd had committed any crime. Anyone could have picked up the discarded piece or wrapping paper and used it to conceal the baby's corpse. They decided to place the house under surveillance and to set up a sting operation. The officers got a young woman to contact Dyer about a child she wanted to put up for adoption. A meeting set up for April 3 (Good Friday). However, when Dyer opened the door that morning expected to find her client and another easy payday, she found instead, four burly detectives.

As the police entered the house they noticed immediately the stench of decomposition, even though no human remains were found. There was, however, plenty of other evidence: including white edging tape; telegrams regarding adoption arrangements; pawn tickets for children's clothing; receipts for classified advertisements and letters from mothers inquiring about the well-being of their children.

The police calculated that in the previous few months alone, at least twenty children had been placed into the care of "Mrs. Thomas," now revealed to be Amelia Dyer. Extrapolating that rate, they estimated that Dyer might have murdered over 400 children in the 25 years she'd been running her baby farming business. They realized too, that they'd caught her just in time. Dyer was preparing to abscond for a new address in Somerset.

Amelia Dyer was arrested on April 4 and charged with murder, her son-in-law, Arthur Palmer, charged as an accessory. During April, the police had the Thames dragged in the area where Helena Fry had been discovered. Six more little corpses were found, including Doris Marmon and Harry Simmons, Dyer's last victims. Each baby had been strangled with white tape, leading Dyer to remark, wryly: "You'll know mine by the tape around their necks."

Evelina Marmon was tracked down and brought to Reading to identify her daughter's remains. It had been 11 days since she'd handed Doris over to Amelia Dyer.

Dyer's trial began at the Old Bailey on 22 May 1896. She entered a guilty plea to a single charge of murder, that of Doris Marmon. This was customary in those days in cases of multiple murder, as it would allow the crown to try her on another charge, should she be acquitted.

But there would be no acquittal in this case. The evidence was overwhelming and the only mitigation Dyer could offer was insanity. Her record of incarceration to various mental institutions was presented by the defense. However, the prosecution successfully argued that such incarcerations always seemed to coincide with times when Dyer was afraid that her crimes might have been exposed.

The insanity plea was never going to work anyway. With the horrendous crimes she'd committed, Dyer was never going to walk free. It took the jury just four and a half minutes to find her guilty. She was sentenced to hang.

In the three weeks she spent in the condemned cell, Dyer filled five exercise books with her "last true and only confession." When the chaplain paid a visit on the night prior to her execution and asked if she had anything to confess, she held up the books, saying, "Isn't this enough?"

Dyer remained, nonetheless, quietly confident that her advanced age would earn her a reprieve. It never came. At 8 am, on Wednesday, June 10, 1896, Amelia Dyer was led from her cell at Newgate Prison. She was escorted up the stairs to the scaffold by James Billington, the public executioner. He guided her to the trapdoors and placed a hood over her head. The noose was positioned around her neck in much the same way as she'd wrapped the edging tape around the throats of her helpless victims. The prison bell had already been tolling for the past fifteen minutes and would continue to do so for another fifteen after the execution had taken place. Crowds had gathered outside, waiting to see the black flag raised on the prison's flagpole. Billington, never one to linger, placed his hand on the lever and opened the trapdoor sending the cold-blooded killer to her richly deserved death.

In the wake of Dyer's execution, new adoption laws were enacted, giving local authorities the power to monitor baby farms and to act on abuse. Newspaper advertisements also came under scrutiny in order to put an end to the trafficking of infants.

But baby trafficking did not stop. Two years after Dyer's death, railway workers found a package on a train traveling from Newton Abbot to Plymouth. Inside was a three-week-old girl, mercifully still alive. She was the daughter of a widow, Jane Hill, who had paid a 'Mrs. Stewart' £12 to take the infant into care. The baby had then simply been dumped on the next train.

Rumor had it that the mysterious Mrs. Stewart was none other than Polly Palmer, Amelia Dyer's daughter.

# Ian Brady and Myra Hindley

*The Moors Murderers*

On October 7, 1965, Superintendent Bob Talbot was about to depart on a two-week holiday with his wife, when he got a call from one of his subordinates at Hyde Police Station in Greater Manchester. Detective Inspector Wills apologized for the intrusion, but explained that there was something he felt warranted the superintendant's attention. He then proceeded to tell Talbot the details of the case, whereupon Talbot departed immediately for the station. Little did he know that he was about to become involved in one of most notorious cases in British criminal history.

When Talbot arrived he was shown into an inquiry room where a distressed young couple was waiting. David Smith, 17, and his wife Maureen then proceeded to tell their story.

The previous night, Smith said, his sister-in-law, Myra Hindley, had visited him at the home he shared with Maureen and her mother. Hindley had told him that she was afraid to walk home in the dark and had asked him to escort her to her residence at 16 Wardle Brook Avenue, Hattersley. When they arrived Hindley asked Smith if he wanted some miniature bottles of wine. Smith said he did, whereupon Hindley told him to wait outside. She said that she'd signal for him to enter the house by flashing the lights once. When the signal came, Smith knocked on the door, which was opened by Ian Brady, Myra's boyfriend. Smith entered the kitchen and was instructed to wait there while Brady fetched the wine he'd been promised.

A few minutes later Smith heard a scream, followed by Hindley shouting for him to come and help. Smith ran to the living room where he saw what at first looked to him like a life-sized rag doll. He soon realized that it was not a doll, but a young man. Ian Brady was standing over the man, an axe in his right hand. The young man groaned, prompting Brady to strike him with the axe. It was silent for a moment, then the man groaned again at which Brady raised the axe high above his head and brought it down in a brutal blow. Then he looped a length of electrical cord around the man's neck and began strangling him while repeating over and over: "You fucking dirty bastard." When the man was finally still, Brady turned to Hindley and said: "That's it, it's the messiest yet."

Leaving the body on the floor, Hindley then made them all a cup of tea, while she and Brady joked about the look on the young man's face when Brady had struck him. They then joked about other victims they'd killed and buried on Saddleworth Moor. Brady had spoken about these murders before, but Smith had always thought that he was joking, indulging in some warped fantasy. He knew now that this was very real, and that his life might be in danger if he didn't play along. When Brady asked him to assist in cleaning up, he agreed, helping Brady and Hindley to wrap the body in plastic and move it to an upstairs bedroom.

Eventually, in the early hours of the morning, he was able to leave, after promising that he'd return next morning to help dispose of the body. As soon as he was out of the house he ran home and woke Maureen. The two of them then phoned the police from a call box and waited to be picked up by a patrol car.

The story sounded almost too bizarre to be true, but of course, it had to be checked out. Superintendent Talbot set off immediately for 16 Wardle Brook Avenue in the company of Detective Sergeant Carr and a backup force of uniformed officers. Talbot didn't want to alarm the suspects, so he donned a delivery uniform before approaching the house and knocking on the front door. When Myra Hindley opened, he identified himself as a police officer and told her he wanted to speak to her boyfriend. He was then led into the living room where Brady was seated. Talbot said that he was investigating "an act of violence involving guns," that had been reported the previous evening. Brady denied any involvement but allowed the police to search the house. When they came to the locked upstairs room, Hindley was asked for the key. She initially said she'd left it at the office, but when Talbot offered to drive her to fetch it, Brady urged her to hand it over. Inside, the police found the body, exactly as Smith had described it. "Eddie and I had a row and the situation got out of hand," Brady said. He was promptly arrested and taken in for questioning.

At the police station, Brady told police that there had been an argument between him, David Smith and the victim, 17-year-old Edward Evans. A fight had ensued during which Smith had hit and kicked Evans several times. He (Brady) had then picked up a hatchet that had been lying on the floor and struck Evans. Hindley was not involved, according to Brady – he and Smith alone had killed Evans. Hindley's story matched Brady's exactly and the police had no reason to disbelieve her.

However, they were very interested in Brady and Hindley's boasts to Smith about the victims they'd murdered and buried on Saddleworth Moor. Over the previous two years, four children, ranging in age from 10 to 16 years, had mysteriously disappeared from the area. Might this case be connected with those disappearances?

Police suspicions were firmed up when they searched 16 Wardle Brook Avenue and found an exercise book with the name of one of the missing children - John Kilbride - written inside. The police also found numerous photos of the moors and uncovered another valuable clue when a twelve-year-old neighbor, Pat Hodge, told them about going to the moors with Brady and Hindley for picnics.

Armed with the photographs and Pat Hodge's directions, the police assembled a search team and began digging. On 10 October 1965, they unearthed the body of 10-year-old Lesley Anne Downey, who had disappeared on December 26, 1964. Eleven days later, 12-year-old John Kilbride was found – he'd been missing since November 11, 1963.

By then, Hindley too had been charged with murder and the police had recovered a treasure trove of evidence from a locker at Manchester Central railway station. Inside a suitcase, was ample evidence of Brady and Hindley's depravity, including nine pornographic photographs of a bound and gagged Lesley Anne Downey, and a truly sickening 13-minute tape-recording of the child screaming and pleading for mercy, while Brady and Hindley taunted and berated her and 'The Little Drummer Boy' played in the background.

As these and other chilling details came to light, the British public was left to ponder what might have created such monsters, who could take pleasure in the sexual abuse and murder of children.

Myra Hindley was born on 23 July 1942 in Gorton, Manchester, the first child of Hettie and Bob Hindley. Her father was serving in a parachute regiment during the first three years of her life, while her mother worked as a machinist, as part of the war effort. Bob had trouble re-adjusting to civilian life after the war and, as both parents worked, Myra was sent to live with her grandmother, Ellen Mayberry.

Myra started school at Peacock Street Primary School at the age of five. She was considered a good pupil, although her attendance record was patchy as her grandmother allowed her to stay home from school on the slightest pretense. Later, she attended Ryder Brow Secondary Modern where her attendance remained poor. Still, she did reasonably well academically and excelled at sports, especially swimming. Not particularly attractive or feminine, she went by the nickname, 'Square Arse' in high school.

Away from the classroom, Myra's reputation as a mature and sensible girl meant that she was a popular babysitter during her teens. She seemed to have a genuine love for children, and parents found her to be capable and trustworthy.

At the age of 15, Myra became friends with Michael Higgins, a timid 13-year-old whom she was very protective towards. She was devastated when he drowned in a local swimming hole, blaming herself for not being there to save him. In the weeks following Michael's death, Myra was inconsolable. She wore black, cried constantly and even converted to Roman Catholicism, Michael's religion. Not long after, she quit school.

Myra's first job was as a clerk at Lawrence Scott, an electrical engineering firm. During this time, she began to change her appearance, bleaching her hair and wearing make-up. She also started attending dances and it was at one of these that she met and became engaged to Ronnie Sinclair, a local boy who worked as a tea blender. However, the engagement did not last long before Myra broke it off. She wanted something more out of life than marriage and kids. She spoke of going to work as a nanny in America and also of joining the army or navy but nothing came of these ambitions.

And then, in January 1961, Myra thought she'd found what she'd been looking for - she met Ian Brady.

Ian Brady was born on 2 January 1938 in the Gorbals, one of Glasgow's toughest ghettos. His mother, Margaret (Peggy) Stewart was a waitress. She never disclosed the name of Ian's father but said he was a journalist for a Glasgow newspaper who had died a few months before the boy's birth.

Unable to raise the baby while holding down a job, Peggy advertised for someone to take Ian into their home. John and Mary Sloane answered the advertisement, and at the age of four months, Ian was unofficially 'adopted' by the couple. Peggy initially visited every Sunday, but as time went by the visits became less and less frequent. Eventually, they stopped altogether. When Ian was 12, Peggy moved with her new husband, Patrick Brady, to Manchester.

The Sloane's were good parents with four children of their own, but from the start they had their hands full with Ian. He was a difficult child, isolated, obstinate, and prone to extreme temper tantrums. At Camden Street Primary School, he was considered bright but indolent. He refused to participate in sports, leading to other boys labeling him a 'sissy.'

At age eleven, Brady passed the entrance exams to Shawlands Academy, a school for gifted children. However, his potential was never realized, as he was lazy and disruptive. He started smoking, gave up on his schoolwork and before long was in trouble with the police. He also developed an obsession with the Nazis, which became his favorite topic of conversation.

Between the ages of 13 and 16, Brady was arrested three times for housebreaking. The third arrest should have resulted in a custodial sentence, but the prosecutor offered a deal – Brady would avoid incarceration if he went to live with his mother in Manchester.

Ian had not seen his mother in four years and had never met his stepfather, Patrick Brady. Nonetheless, Peggy agreed to take him in and, in 1954, he moved south.

Brady had always felt like an outsider and the move to Manchester only exacerbated that. He attempted to blend in with his new family by changing his name from Stewart to Brady and by accepting the job that his stepfather found for him as a porter at a local market. Still, his feelings of isolation persisted and he found solace in books - Dostoyevsky's Crime and Punishment, the Marquis de Sade, Justine, The Kiss of the Whip, and The Torture Chamber.

When he wasn't reading sadistic literature, Brady was committing petty larcenies. Shortly after quitting his job at the market and starting work at a brewery, he was arrested for stealing from his employer. He was sentenced to a borstal (an institution for young offenders) for two years. Later, after a drunken scuffle with a guard, he was sent to a much tougher prison. But something useful did come out of his incarceration. He managed to study for a bookkeeping qualification.

After his release in November 1957, Brady was unemployed for several months before he obtained work as a laborer. In 1959, he decided to put his bookkeeping skills to use and found employment as a stock clerk with Millwards Merchandising. A little more than a year later, Myra Hindley joined the same company as a secretary.

Myra was immediately smitten by the sullen Brady, who she thought of as "enigmatic, worldly, and intelligent." She began keeping a diary in which she wrote of her intense longing for Brady. For his part, he remained steadfastly disinterested.

A year after they'd begun working together, Brady, under the influence of a few drinks at the company Christmas party, asked Hindley for a date. She readily accepted. Whether or not Brady had decided to indoctrinate Hindley into his secret world at this time, is unknown. What we do know is that their first date was to a showing of "The Nuremberg Trials." Over the weeks that followed, he played her records of Nazi marching songs and encouraged her to read some of his favorite books - Mein Kampf, Crime and Punishment, and de Sade. Hindley, smitten with the dangerous, brooding Brady happily complied. He became her first lover and she was soon soaking up all of his twisted philosophical theories. She even changed her appearance and began dressing in long boots and mini skirts, with bleached hair and dark make-up. Although previously lacking in sexual experience she allowed him to take pornographic photographs of her.

Encouraged by Hindley's absolute devotion to him, Brady began initiating her into his more extreme and paranoid ideologies. By the time he proffered the idea that rape and murder were not wrong, that murder was in fact, the supreme pleasure, Myra barely flinched. She was totally under his influence. Not only that, but she'd come to accept these ideas as her own. In effect, their personalities had become fused.

But there is a world of difference between accepting an idea in principle and actually carrying it out. Early in 1963, Brady decided to put Hindley's devotion to the test. He began speaking of robbing a bank and told her he would need her as a get-away driver. Hindley immediately began taking driving lessons, joined a rifle club and purchased two guns. The robbery was never carried out, but Brady knew now that Myra was ready. On the night of 12 July 1963, the warped, killer couple took their first victim.

That night, Brady instructed Hindley to drive her van around the area while he followed on his motorcycle. When he spotted a victim he would flash his headlight, and Hindley was then to stop and offer the person a lift.

As they drove along Gorton Lane, Brady saw a girl of about seven or eight walking towards them. He signaled Hindley to stop, but she continued driving past the girl. Brady then caught up to her and angrily demanded to know why she hadn't offered the girl a lift. Hindley said it was because the girl was a near neighbor of her mother. In truth, she was worried above the uproar that the disappearance of such a young child would cause.

Just after 8:00 pm, Brady spotted a girl walking along Froxmer Street. She was a wearing a pale blue coat and white high-heeled shoes. Brady again flashed his headlights indicating for Hindley to stop. This time, she complied. Hindley recognized the girl as Pauline Reade, a 16-year-old friend of her younger sister, Maureen. Pauline said she was on her way to a dance at the British Railways Club in Gorton, but agreed to drive with Hindley to Saddleworth Moor, to search for an expensive glove Hindley said she'd lost there.

Hindley brought the van to a stop along a desolate stretch of road and waited as Brady pulled in behind on his motorcycle. Hindley introduced him as her boyfriend, and said that he was also there to help search for the missing glove. Brady then took Pauline onto the moor while Hindley waited in the van. About 30 minutes later, he returned alone, and told Hindley to follow him. He led her back to the spot where Pauline lay dying, her throat cut. He told her to watch Pauline while he fetched a spade he'd hidden nearby on a previous visit to the moor. When he returned, he dug a shallow grave and buried the girl. They then loaded the motorcycle into the back of the van and drove home together. On the way they passed Pauline's mother, Joan, searching the streets for her daughter.

Just over four months later, on November 23, 1963, Brady and Hindley were trawling for another victim when they encountered 12-year-old John Kilbride at a market in Ashton-under-Lyne. They offered him a lift home, which the boy willingly accepted. On the way there Brady suggested they make a detour to the moors to look for a lost glove. He promised John a bottle of sherry in exchange for his help. Hindley again waited in the car while Brady led the child out onto the moor. After sexually assaulting the boy, he tried to kill him by cutting his throat. When that failed, he strangled him to death with a shoelace.

The killers waited eight months before taking their next victim, another twelve-year-old. On the evening of June 16, 1964, Keith Bennett was on his way to his grandmother's house in Longsight when he encountered Brady and Hindley. They asked him to help them load some boxes, promising to bring him home straight after. As with the other victims, Keith was then driven to Saddleworth Moor on the pretext of looking for a lost glove. While Hindley stayed in the car, Brady left with the boy, returning alone 30 minutes later. He told Hindley that he'd sexually assaulted the boy before strangling him with a piece of string.

On December 26, Brady and Hindley spotted 10-year-old Lesley Ann Downey at a fairground. When they were sure that the child was alone, they approached her and asked her to help them carry some shopping to their car. They then offered the girl a lift home but stopped off first at their house. Once Leslie Ann was inside she was undressed, gagged and bound, and then forced to pose for pornographic photographs. She was then raped before being strangled to death with a piece of string. Hindley claimed afterwards that she went to fill a bath for Leslie Ann and came back to find Brady had killed her. However, according to Brady, Hindley was an active participant and it was she who killed the little girl, strangling her with her bare hands.

While it will probably never be established who actually killed Leslie Ann, the tape recording later found by the police clearly proves that Hindley was a lot more involved than she claims.

The following morning Brady and Hindley drove to Saddleworth Moor, where the buried Leslie Ann's tiny corpse in a shallow grave.

On 6 October 1965, Brady picked up 17-year-old apprentice engineer Edward Evans at Manchester Central railway station and invited him to his home at 16 Wardle Brook Avenue, where Brady beat him to death with an axe. At the time of this murder, Brady had been grooming Hindley's 17-year-old brother-in-law, David Smith, for over a year. Smith was in awe of the older man and Brady hoped to turn him into another of his disciples. However,

Brady miscalculated badly in trying to involve Smith in the Evans murder. Smith was sickened by what he saw and went to the police.

Ian Brady and Myra Hindley were brought to trial at Chester Assizes on April 27, 1966. Despite protestations of innocence, Brady was found guilty of the murders of Lesley Ann Downey, John Kilbride, and Edward Evans. Hindley was found guilty of the murders of Lesley Ann Downey and Edward Evans. The death penalty had been abolished just months before their trial so they escaped that fate, although such was the public revulsion at their crimes that there were calls to reinstate capital punishment. The two heartless killers were sentenced instead to life imprisonment.

The story didn't end there, though. Ten years into her sentence, Hindley began a protracted fight to secure her freedom. Despite garnering a number of high profile supporters to her cause, this would ultimately prove unsuccessful as a succession of Home Secretaries blocked the move. Given the depth of public opinion against Brady and Hindley, releasing her would have amounted to political suicide. Myra Hindley died on November 15, 2002. She was 60 years old and had been in prison for 35 years.

By contrast, Ian Brady never sought freedom. In fact, he issued a statement via his solicitor stating: "I accept that the weight of the crimes Myra and I were convicted of justifies permanent imprisonment, regardless of expressed personal remorse and verifiable change."

In October 1999, while housed at the high-security Ashworth Psychiatric Hospital, Brady went on a hunger strike saying that he would rather die than "rot slowly" in prison. After refusing food he was force fed with a tube by hospital staff. Brady subsequently fought a long legal battle trying to secure the right to end his life. His initial action was dismissed and all subsequent appeals were been defeated. At time of writing he remains incarcerated at Ashworth.

# Graham Young

## The St. Albans Poisoner

*"It grew on me like drug habit, except it was not me who was taking the drugs." – Graham Young*

In February 1961, a peculiar illness started afflicting the Young household in north London. It began with 37-year-old Molly Young suffering bouts of vomiting and diarrhea along with excruciating stomach pains. Then, her husband Fred, 44, began experiencing similar symptoms and Fred's daughter Winifred, 22, also became violently ill. Finally, Graham, at 14 the youngest member of the family, succumbed to the mystery bug. And it didn't stop there. Before long the affliction had spread beyond the immediate family. Several of Graham's school friends were ill with similarly painful symptoms.

For nine long months the Young family enduring their illness, passing between them various theories as to its source. Then, in November 1961, things took a more serious turn. Winifred Young was on her way to work when she began suffering hallucinations and had to be rushed from the train to hospital. The doctors who examined her were mystified - Winifred appeared to have been poisoned with a rare form of Belladonna.

The doctors may have been puzzled, but when Fred Young heard the prognosis, it immediately made sense to him. His son Graham was obsessed with chemistry and was always messing around with some or other concoction. It now seemed clear to Fred that Graham had somehow, inadvertently, contaminated the family's food.

He confronted his son with this theory, but Graham denied it. He blamed Winifred, who he said had been mixing shampoo in the family's teacups. Unconvinced, Fred searched Graham's room but found nothing incriminating. Nevertheless, he warned his son to be more careful in future.

Graham's interest in chemistry had begun at an early age. He was not yet 10-years-old when he'd begun stealing his stepmother's nail varnish and perfumes in order to analyze the contents. By 11, he could recite the components of various headache pills and cough medicines, and would joyously warn of the symptoms of overdosing on them. He spent hours at the library poring over books on his favorite subject. By the time he was 13, Graham had already acquired a level of knowledge similar to that of a chemistry post-graduate.

But Graham's fascination with chemistry went beyond mere schoolboy inquisitiveness. He had a particular interest in poisons, was known to carry a bottle of acid with him and had once constructed a bomb that had destroyed a neighbor's wall. Still, Fred couldn't believe that his son would deliberately be poisoning his family. Before long, he'd have cause to re-evaluate that belief.

Graham Young was born in Neasden, northwest London on September 7, 1947. His mother, Margaret, developed pleurisy during the pregnancy, and although she delivered a healthy baby, she died of tuberculosis just three months after the birth. Devastated by her death and unable to cope with two young children, Fred Young sent Graham to live with his Aunt Winnie, while 8-year-old Winifred was taken in by her grandmother.

Then, when Graham was two-and-a-half, Fred remarried and reunited his family, this time with their new stepmother, Molly.

We will never know what effect these early upheavals may have had on the boy, but from an early age Graham Young showed signs that he was different. Where other boys idolized football players and pop stars, his heroes were murders like Crippen and William Palmer. Where other kids read comic books and teen magazines, his favorite reading was a book called "Sixty Famous Trials," especially the chapters on infamous poisoners.

If that wasn't enough, he began developing an unhealthy interest in the Nazis. From the age of about 12, he began talking openly about his admiration for Adolf Hitler. He also developed a fascination with the occult and claimed to be part of a local coven run by a man he had met at the library.

At school, Graham was a solitary child. Most of his classmates found him "creepy," while he hardly endeared himself to teachers by wearing a swastika badge on his uniform. World War II had ended only 15 years before, for many who had lost friends and loved ones the wounds were still fresh.

Graham was an intelligent boy, but he showed little interest in his studies. The one exception was chemistry, in which his fascination bordered on obsession. Most afternoons he could be found at the library, poring over books on the subject, particularly ones on toxicology, the study of poisons.

At home, Graham spent much of his time alone in his room dabbling with one or other experiment. His relationship with his father appears to have been distant, while he openly admitted to his classmates how much he hated his stepmother. He'd show them a small plasticine figure, stuck full of pins, and claim it was a voodoo doll representing Molly. On one occasion, after Molly reprimanded him for some or other infraction, he drew a picture of a tombstone, on which he wrote: "In Hateful Memory of Molly Young, RIP." He then deliberately left it out where she would see it.

The first person to be subjected to Graham Young's experiments with poison was a boy named Christopher Williams, who had befriended Young due to a mutual interest in science. Williams was a neighbor of the Young family and he and Graham would often eat lunch together at school, sometimes swapping sandwiches. It wasn't long before Christopher began suffering from headaches, vomiting, and painful stomach cramps. His mother at first thought he was play-acting in order to stay home from school, but eventually, she took him to a doctor who diagnosed a migraine. No one considered poison, after all, how would a 13-year-old get his hands on dangerous toxins?

Graham Young had, though, using his detailed knowledge of poisons to convince two local pharmacists that he was 17 and needed the substances for his studies. Using this ruse, he managed to a build up a substantial stash of antimony, arsenic, digitalis, and thallium – enough, it was later calculated, to kill 300 people.

Still, he stuck to relatively small doses with Christopher Williams, and despite Williams knowing about his friend's obsession with poisons he apparently never suspected him. For his part, Graham did a good job of playing the concerned buddy, even if he seemed overly eager to hear Christopher's descriptions of his pain and suffering.

Luckily for Williams, Young soon tired of torturing him. The problem was that Christopher's frequent absences from school made it impossible for Graham to monitor his symptoms. He needed subjects who he could observe at close quarters, so he turned his attention to those nearest to him - his own family.

During the early months of 1962, Molly Young's health deteriorated steadily. She lost weight, suffered excruciating backache, and began losing her hair. She also appeared to age noticeably. Then her symptoms changed suddenly. On Easter

Saturday, 1962, she woke up with stiffness in her neck muscles and the sensation of pins and needles in her hands and feet. Despite feeling unwell, Molly went out shopping, while Fred Young went for a drink at the local pub. When Fred returned home at around lunchtime, he found Graham standing transfixed at the kitchen window, staring out into the back garden. Following his son's gaze, Fred saw Molly writhing in agony on the grass. She died in hospital later that day.

Molly Young's death was put down to the prolapse of a bone at the top of the spinal column (a common symptom of antimony poisoning although no one seemed to make the connection at the time). However, it would later emerge that this was not the cause of death. Graham had, in fact, been feeding antimony to Molly for so long that she'd built up a tolerance to the poison. Frustrated that the antimony was no longer having any effect, Young changed his poison of choice. On the night prior to her death, he'd spiked Molly's evening meal with 20 grains of thallium, a colorless, odorless, tasteless 'heavy metal.' He overdid it somewhat – 20 grams is enough to kill five people.

One might think that the death of his stepmother would have frightened Graham out of conducting further 'experiments,' instead, it seems to have spurred him on. Several of the extended Young family suffered vomiting and diarrhea after eating the sandwiches provided after the funeral. And Graham had already switched his attention to his next victim – his grieving father.

Fred Young had suffered occasional vomiting, diarrhea, and stomach cramps during Molly's illness, but after her death, the symptoms intensified to such an extent that he eventually had to be hospitalized. Graham visited him frequently but spent most of his time enthusiastically discussing Fred's condition and symptoms with the doctors. Eventually, antimony poisoning was diagnosed. But if Fred suspected that Graham was responsible, he didn't say. The idea that his own son might be the cause of his torment (and possibly the death of his wife) must have been too horrendous to contemplate.

It took an outsider to draw the authorities' attention to Graham Young. Geoffrey Hughes, Graham's chemistry teacher, had long been uneasy about the boy's behavior and bizarre utterings. Eventually, he decided to search Graham's desk and was shocked at what he found there – bottles of poisons, juvenile sketches of dying men, essays about infamous poisoners. Hughes took his findings to the police.

A few days later, Young was called into, what he thought was, a careers interview. The interviewer (in reality a police psychiatrist) began by asking Young about his interests and then encouraged him to talk about his expertise with poisons. Needless to say, Young took to this like a duck to water, leaving the interviewer shocked and horrified with some of his pronouncements. Yet, when the true intent of the interview was revealed, Young initially denied everything. Eventually, though, he broke down and confessed, before leading officers to his various caches of poisons.

Although there was insufficient evidence to try the 14-year-old for the murder of his stepmother, he was convicted of poisoning his father, sister, and friend, Chris Williams. He was sent to Broadmoor maximum-security hospital with an order that he was not to be released without the permission of the Home Secretary for 15 years. He would be the youngest inmate to be incarcerated at Broadmoor since 1885.

And he soon made his mark. A few weeks after his arrival at the hospital, a fellow prisoner named John Berridge died of cyanide poisoning. Young had been heard complaining about Berridge and his loud snoring in the communal dorms. The authorities were baffled. There was no cyanide anywhere in the prison, so how had Berrige ingested it? Young was quick to enlighten them. Cyanide can be extracted from laurel bush leaves, he said, and there are plenty growing in the adjoining fields. It sounded suspiciously like a confession but, for whatever reason, it wasn't followed up. Berrige's death was ruled a suicide.

A number of other suspicious incidents occurred during Young's stay at Broadmoor. On one occasion the staff's coffee was found to be contaminated with bleach, on another, a quantity of toxic sugar soap (a substance used to wash down walls prior to painting) was found in a tea urn.

Young also kept up his earlier interest in Nazism, growing a Hitler mustache and making hundreds of wooden swastikas. While these hardly appear the actions of a man working towards ridding himself of the demons that plagued him, Young was in other respects a model prisoner. After serving 5 years, he was moved to a less secure block. At 8 years, the prison psychiatrist, Dr. Edgar Udwin, petitioned the Home Secretary for his release, stating confidently that Young was "no longer obsessed with poisons, violence and mischief."

Sensing his imminent release, Young wrote to his sister Winifred, joking: "Your friendly neighborhood Frankenstein will soon be at liberty." To one of the Broadmoor nurses he said: "When I get out, I'm going to kill one person for every year I've spent in this place."

Incredibly, this apparently genuine threat never reached the ears of the authorities. Young was released on February 4, 1971. After staying with Winifred and her husband Dennis for a week, Young moved to a hostel in Slough. Soon after his arrival, fellow resident Trevor Sparkes, 34, began experiencing sharp pains in his stomach. Young suggested that a glass of wine might help, but this only made things worse. Sparks began vomiting and suffering diarrhea. His face swelled and he began experiencing pains in his scrotum. Eventually, Sparkes collapsed while playing a game of soccer. He was rushed to hospital, but doctors couldn't diagnose the problem. He continued suffering terrible pains for years after. Another hostel dweller began experiencing similar symptoms after going out for a drink with Young. This man endured such agonizing pain that he ended up taking his own life.

Young, meanwhile, had found employment as a store clerk at John Hadland Ltd, a photographic company in Bovingdon, Hertfordshire. In lieu of references, he referred his new employer to Dr. Udwin, the Broadmoor psychiatrist. Udwin wrote back with assurances that Young had made a full recovery from the personality disorder that had plagued him. No mention was made of his love of poisons, which is astounding given the many toxic chemicals stored on the premises of his new employer.

As it turned out, Young had no need of the toxins available on site. He had already armed himself with a stash of antimony and thallium, obtained using a fake ID, from a London pharmacist.

Young made friends quickly at Hadland, first with 41-year-old Ron Hewitt, whose job he was taking over, then with 59-year-old storeroom manager Bob Egle and 60-year-old stock supervisor Fred Biggs. It wasn't long before Egle started feeling ill and began to take time off work. Then, Ron Hewitt developed diarrhea, sharp abdominal pains and a burning sensation in the throat after drinking a cup of tea brought to him by Young. The symptoms subsided after a few days at home but resumed immediately after he returned to work.

Hewitt left the company soon after and suffered no further symptoms. Bob Egle, too, recovered after taking a holiday. However, the day after returning to work, the mystery illness was back. His fingers became numb, and he couldn't move without agonizing pain. By the time he was rushed to hospital, he was virtually paralyzed, and unable to speak. He died 10 days later, on July 7, 1971, the cause of death given as bronchial pneumonia.

Of all the Hadland employees, Graham Young seemed most affected by Egle's death, so much so that he was chosen to accompany the managing director to the cremation.

In the weeks following the death, the staff at Hadland tried to put the tragic incident behind them. However, Young seemed unprepared to let it go. He mused endlessly about the possible medical causes of Egle's symptoms. Then in September 1971, Fred

Biggs began to suffer the similar symptoms. And the illness also spread to other staff members.

One of Young's colleagues in the storeroom, Jethro Batt, 39, accepted a cup of coffee from Young one evening but threw it away because it tasted bitter. "What's the matter?" Young smirked. "Do you think I'm trying to poison you?" A short while later, Batt started throwing up and experienced intense pain in his legs. Peter Buck and David Tilson also suffered. Batt and Tilson started losing clumps of hair, giving them the appearance, in the words of a doctor of, "three-quarter plucked chickens."

Other staff members displayed different symptoms. Receptionist, Diana Smart, complained of suffering from foul smelling feet, while Buck and Tilson found themselves rendered impotent. These and other ailments were put down to some kind of virus, which became known locally as "the Bovingdon Bug." A number of local residents had indeed been afflicted with a stomach bug over the preceding few months and this provided Young with a fortuitous cover.

After toning down his activities for a short while, the poisoner was back with a vengeance. Jethro Batt fell ill again, his pain so extreme that he had to be hospitalized. Fred Biggs suffered even worse symptoms, his skin began to peel off, and he was in so much pain that he could not stand the weight of a bed sheet on his body. When death finally came on November 19, it must have seemed a merciful release.

The company directors were at a loss to explain what had killed two employees in such a short time. On the afternoon that Fred Biggs' death was announced, they brought in a doctor to assure staff that there was no evidence that hygiene on the company premises could have caused the deaths and illnesses. Yet, even as the doctor concluded his statement, a hand shot up at the back of the room. Graham Young wanted to know whether the doctor had considered thallium poisoning as a possible cause and provided a detailed explanation on why he thought this might be the case. The doctor was puzzled by Young's questions and told the company's managing director about them. He, in turn, informed the police.

It didn't take long for detectives to figure out that the outbreak of illnesses had started shortly after Young had begun working at Hadland. A brief conversation with their forensic colleagues confirmed that the symptoms of the victims were consistent with thallium poisoning. A quick background check uncovered Graham Young's past as a convicted poisoner. A search of Young's room turned up bottles, vials, and tubes of various poisons, plus a ledger in which Young had cataloged in great detail the sufferings and symptoms of his subjects, even including graphs to determine when they might expire. An entry written the day before Fred Biggs died read: "'F' is responding to treatment. He is being obstinately difficult. If he survives a third week he will live. I am most annoyed."

On Saturday, November 21, 1971, Young was visiting his father and Aunt Winnie in Sheerness, Kent, when police officers arrived to arrest him. After they had left with Graham in custody, Fred Young gathered Graham's birth certificate and every other document relating to his son and tore them to shreds.

Under interrogation, Young quickly confessed to the poisonings. He even boasted of having committed "the perfect murder" of his stepmother in 1962. He refused to sign a statement admitting his guilt, though. He was intent on having his day in court, and of exploiting his notoriety to the full

Graham Young went on trial at St. Albans Crown Court in June 1972. Young was confident, cocky even, believing he couldn't be prosecuted because Bob Egle had been cremated, thus destroying evidence of thallium poisoning. In the case of Fred Biggs, he insisted that he'd given Fred some thallium grains to help him kill bugs in his garden. Biggs must have ingested those accidently. He also explained away the diary, claiming it was research he was doing for a novel he planned to write.

But, Young reckoned without advances in forensic science. Experts were able to find traces of thallium in Bob Egle's ashes. Fred Biggs' wife also confirmed that he never used thallium on his garden, while Young's claim about the diary being a research document was proven to be ludicrous, given some of the excerpts.

Young was convicted of two murders, two attempted murders, and two counts of administering poison. He was sentenced to four terms of life imprisonment, to be served in the maximum security Parkhurst prison. He died there in 1990, aged just 42. The cause of death was given as a heart attack, although many believe that he managed to poison one final victim - himself.

# Robert Black

*Child Killer*

Robert Black was born in Grangemouth, some 20 miles from Edinburgh, on 21 April 1947. His parents were unmarried, his mother, Jessie, even declining to record the father's name on the boy's birth certificate. Within days of Robert's birth, Jessie decided to put him up for adoption. He was taken in by Jack and Margaret Tulip, a couple in their fifties who had fostered several children before. Black would spend eleven years in this foster home although Jack Tulip died when Robert was 5-years-old. He would later say that he has no recall of the first five years of his life, but those who remember him from those days say that he was frequently heavily bruised as a child.

At school, Robert was called 'Smelly Robbie Tulip' by his classmates and was known as a loner, who preferred the company of younger kids. He also developed a reputation as a bully, on one occasion severely beating a disabled boy for no apparent reason.

The local bobby also flagged him as a bit of a ruffian, but in the main Black confined himself to acts of petty violence, and avoided more serious trouble.

But there were things neither the bobby, nor Robert's classmates nor Margaret Tulip saw, signs of an aberrant persona in the making. By the age of eight, Black was already developing a precocious sexual self-awareness. Years later he'd relate to officers, his habit of inserting objects into anus, an obsessive practice he'd continue throughout his life. He also began to believe that he should have been born a girl.

However, he was by no means homosexual in his desires. Black vividly recalled an experience when, at age five, he and a little girl undressed to look at each other's sexual parts. He also remembered attending Highland Dance classes, when he'd lie on the floor and try to get a look up the girl's skirts. He was just seven at the time.

In 1958, Margaret Tulip died, depriving the 11-year-old Black of a mother for the second time. Another local couple offered to take him in, but it was decided that he would go to the Redding Children's Home near Falkirk. Here, aged 12, Black made a first inept attempt at rape. The girl, who was a similar age, reported the incident and Black was packed off to the all-male Red House reformatory in Musselburgh. He became a target for bullies at Musselburgh. He also later claimed he was frequently forced to perform oral sex on a male staff member.

In the summer of 1962 when Black was fifteen, he left Red House and got a job in Greenock as a delivery boy. Black soon put his delivery route to good use, molesting between 30 and 40 young girls over the next year. Amazingly, none of these attacks was reported, although Black's luck would eventually run out in 1963, when he was 17. The charge was 'lewd and libidinous' behavior with a minor. In truth, it should have been attempted murder.

Black had approached the seven-year-old girl in a park and asked her if she wanted to see some kittens. After the girl trustingly followed him to a deserted building, he strangled her into unconsciousness, then removed her underwear and inserted his finger in her vagina. He then masturbated over the child's inert body before leaving her lying unconscious on the floor. She was found later, wandering the streets - bleeding, crying and confused.

The sentence for this attack was astonishingly lenient, amounting to no more than a reprimand. Nonetheless, Black was ordered by Social Services to leave Greenock. He returned to Grangemouth, where he got a job with a builders' supply company and met his first (and only) girlfriend. The relationship with Pamela Hodgson lasted several months and was serious enough for the couple to discuss marriage. Eventually, though, Pamela called it off, leaving Black devastated.

Although Black claims that while he and Pamela were together, he did not molest any girls, he was forced to leave Grangemouth for exactly that reason. First, it was the nine-year-old granddaughter of his landlady, which, although charges were not pressed, led to him losing both his quarters and his job. Then, he molested a seven-year-old and was found guilty of three counts of indecent assault. He was sentenced to a year at a juvenile detention center.

Upon his release, in March 1968, Black left Scotland and headed south, to the anonymity of London. Over the next decade, he avoided any criminal convictions. However, his fixation with young girls had found a new outlet. He began compiling a massive collection of child pornography, obtained clandestinely from mainland Europe. When Black's room was eventually searched after his arrest, the police discovered hundreds of magazines, as well as over 50 videotapes.

Still, on the surface, Black maintained a somewhat normal façade. He enjoyed swimming and football and was often found playing darts at the local pub. Eddie and Kathy Rayson, from whom he rented an attic room, remember him as, "a perfect tenant who always paid the rent on time and never caused any problems." The Rayson's kids, though, had a nickname for Black - they called him 'Smelly Bob.'

In 1976, Black found employment as a driver for to a company called Poster Dispatch and Storage (PDS). His job involved delivering posters to various depots around England and Scotland. Black enjoyed the solitude that the work allowed him and was a good employee. He spent the next ten years at PDS, his tenure ending when he was fired due to a string of minor car accidents. Fortunately for Black, his dismissal coincided with two former employees buying out the company and he was re-employed. He continued to get into accidents, but he was a hard worker and was always keen to take on the longer runs that other drivers avoided, such as London to Scotland.

Black would later reveal that he carried various masturbatory tools with him on these trips and continued to fantasize about touching little girls. One fantasy that he returned to again and again was of the seven-year-old girl that he'd molested and left for dead in the abandoned building. That assault was replayed and embellished upon in Black's mind so many times that eventually the need to act on it became all but overwhelming. It was then that Robert Black crossed the line to murder.

On the afternoon of 31 July 1982, 11-year-old Susan Maxwell set off on foot to a tennis game she was going to play with her friend, Alison Raeburn. Susan had asked if she could cycle to the game, but her mother, Liz, was worried about traffic and suggested that Susan walk instead. The Maxwell's lived in Cornhill-on-Tweed, a small village on the English side of the English/Scottish border. Susan's tennis game was on the Scottish side, in Coldstream. As it turned out, Susan didn't end up walking to her game after all – a farm-worker going into Coldstream gave her a ride.

At around four o'clock Liz decided to drive to Coldstream and pick Susan up. It was a hot day and she figured that, after playing tennis for an hour, Susan wouldn't be too keen on the long walk home. Liz expected to encounter Susan on route, but she drove all the way to the Lennel Tennis Club without seeing her. Slightly concerned, she turned around and headed for home, thinking she'd probably missed Susan along the road. By the time she got back home with still no sight of her daughter, her concerned had been elevated to near panic. Then, when a call to Alison established that Susan had indeed started on her way home, Liz immediately called the police.

Officers were quickly on the scene, retracing Susan's movements and questioning people on route. Many people had seen Susan that afternoon, but one consistent pattern began to emerge from their statements. It appeared that Susan had disappeared shortly after crossing the Tweed Bridge back into England. Several people had seen her crossing the bridge at around half past four. Then, as if by magic, she was gone.

A search was launched, involving the Northumbria police and volunteers making up about a third of the village of Cornhill. Susan's father, Fordyce, went out every day with the search parties. They found nothing. Then, on Friday, August 13, about two weeks after Susan disappearance, Liz and Fordyce were on a local radio program appealing for information when they received the news they'd been dreading. A man named Arthur Meadows had found Susan's body. It was in a ditch next to the A518 road at Loxley, 250 miles from where Susan had been abducted. After two weeks out in the warm weather, decomposition was so advanced that it was only possible to identify her from dental records. It was impossible to determine cause of death, but her shorts had been removed, suggesting a sexual motive to the crime.

As Susan's body was found in Staffordshire, responsibility for the case fell to the Staffordshire police, although they worked closely with the Northumbria force. Yet an intensive investigation, extending over 12 months and resulting in the accumulation of over 500,000 hand-written index cards of information, turned up nothing.

On July 8, 1983, almost a year after the murder of Susan Maxwell, five-year-old Caroline Hogg disappeared from a park near her home in Portobello, a suburb of Edinburgh. On the day of her disappearance, Caroline had been to a friend's birthday party and had walked to a bus stop with her mother, Annette, to see her grandmother off. When they returning home at around 7 p.m. Annette had begged her mother to let her go to the park for a few minutes play before bedtime. It was not unusual for Caroline to go to the playground alone. It was just a short walk from the house and the small community where they lived was very safe. Besides, Caroline knew not to talk to strangers or to venture beyond the park to the promenade or the permanent fairground, Fun City.

At 7.15 Annette, who had told Caroline to return in five minutes, sent her son Stuart to look for his sister. When Stuart returned, saying he was unable to find her, Annette went herself. Soon the whole family was out searching and at around eight o'clock, Annette called the police. As with Susan Maxwell, many people had seen the little girl that night. Disconcertingly, most of the sightings were of Caroline in the company of a scruffy-looking man. The man was seen watching her as she played at the park, then leading her towards the fairground and paying for her to ride the children's roundabout. They were last seen walking away from Fun City, hand-in-hand.

Another massive hunt was launched, involving as many as 2,000 police and volunteers. It continued for over a week and turned up nothing. Like the Maxwells the Hoggs took to the radio begging for their daughter's return, a tear-choked Annette crying, "Please, let her come home. We really miss her. I really miss her."

Caroline's tiny corpse was found on July 18 in a lay-by at Twycross in Leicestershire, Her body had been left 300 miles from where she had been taken but was found just 24 miles from that of Susan Maxwell. As in the previous case, decomposition was severe, making it impossible to determine cause of death. The motive seemed obvious, though; Caroline's body was completely naked.

There were obvious similarities between the murders of Susan and Caroline, leading the police to believe that the same man was responsible. It was therefore decided that the four forces involved (Northumbria, Staffordshire, Edinburgh and Leicestershire would form a joint task force under Deputy Chief Constable Hector Clark of Northumbria. Clark's first move was to request that all the data from the two murders be entered into a computer. However, the sheer volume of information from the Susan Maxwell investigation rendered this impractical given available resources. It was therefore decided that data from the Caroline Hogg inquiry would be fed into the database, while the Susan Maxwell data would remain on index cards.

Every aspect of the two crimes was re-examined and revisited, witnesses re-questioned, house-to-house enquiries made. Officers sat at the side of the A444 highway for weeks recording the license plates of cars that passed. Meanwhile, every jurisdiction in the country was asked to draw up a list of possible suspects; parking tickets issued near the crime scene were examined; holiday-makers from as far away as Australia were asked to send in film or video they'd taken at Fun City on the night of Caroline's disappearance. It was a diligently executed operation, but it yielded no clues. Eventually, the trail went cold. It would remain so for three years.

At around 8 p.m. on 26 March 1986, Jacki Harper asked if one of her children would go to go to the corner shop to buy a loaf of bread. Ten-year-old Sarah volunteered, accepting £1 from her mother and picking up two empty lemonade bottles on her way out.

The K&M Store, where Sarah was headed, was just over a hundred yards from the Harper's home in Morley, Leeds. Sarah should have been there and back in five minutes. When she hadn't returned by 8.15, Jacki started to worry, although she thought that Sarah was probably just dawdling and sent Sarah's sister, Claire, to look for her. When Claire returned and said she couldn't find Sarah, the family got into their car and drove around the neighborhood looking for her. At nine o'clock the police were called.

It was soon established that Sarah had been at K & M to make her purchase. She'd also redeemed the deposit on the lemonade bottles and bought two packets of crisps. She left the shop at five past eight and shortly afterwards was seen by two girls who knew her, taking a short cut through an alley. Then, like Susan and Caroline, she simply disappeared.

On 19 April, a man named David Moult was walking his dog along the River Trent in Nottingham when he spotted something floating in the river. At first, he thought it was a piece of sacking, but then the current turned it over and he realized that it was a body. Using a stick, Moult managed to pull the body to the riverbank. He then called the police. It was later determined that Sarah Harper had been put into the water while she was still alive. The injuries to her vagina and anus, which had been inflicted pre-mortem, were described by the pathologist as "terrible."

Initially, the police did not believe that the murder of Sarah Harper was connected to those of Susan Maxwell and Caroline Hogg. The case was assigned to Detective Superintendent John Stainthorpe of the West Yorkshire police who set about making painstaking enquiries in the area where Sarah was abducted. This yielded a number of clues, including a description of a strange man seen lurking in the vicinity of the K & M Store, and a white van seen parked nearby.

The police also had a new weapon at their disposal. A computer system called HOLMES (Home Office Large Major Enquiry System), which had been set up after the Yorkshire Ripper case. The system was designed to log, process, gather and analyze information. From day one, all info related to the Sarah Harper investigation was entered into the database.

Despite this new technological, however, the police were getting no further in their investigation. No matter how sophisticated HOLMES was, if the name of the offender wasn't stored in its memory banks, it was useless.

Eight months into the Sarah Harper inquiry the police were no closer to identifying the killer. It was then decided that the three cases would be linked together and that a single database would be established. This was a massive undertaking, one that would eventually take three years to complete. Yet, when the break came in the case it was not as a result of technology but a stroke of luck, a miscalculation on the part of the killer.

On 14 July 1990, a sunny day in the village of Stow close to the Scottish border, six-year-old Mandy Wilson was on her way to a friend's house to play. One of Mandy's neighbors, David Herkes, was mowing his lawn as Mandy passed. He noticed a white van parked at the curb a bit further down the road, its passenger door open. As Herkes bent down to look at his mower blades, all he could see was Mandy's feet. Suddenly, they vanished and as Herkes stood up, he saw a man trying to stuff something under the dashboard of the van. Then the man got into the vehicle and raced off.

David Herkes had the presence of mind to take down the van's license plate number before he ran to call the police. Officers were quickly on the scene and a broadcast went out for patrol cars to be on the lookout for the white van. Then, as Herkes was telling the police and the girl's distraught father what had happened, he spotted the van driving back up the road. "That's him!" he shouted and an officer ran into the road and forced the van to a stop.

The driver, who identified himself as Robert Black, was quickly cuffed and arrested, while officers fought to restrain Mandy's father from attacking him. Meanwhile, a search of the van turned up the little girl, terrified but alive. Her hands were tied and she'd been pushed into a sleeping bag that was shoved into the passenger foot-well. A later examination proved that the little girl had been sexually assaulted. Still, she'd had a lucky escape.

Robert Black's came to trial on 10 August 1990. The evidence against him was overwhelming and he had little choice but to plead guilty. He was sentenced to life imprisonment, the judge adding that his release would not be considered "until such time as it is safe to do so."

But Black had more to answer for than the abduction and assault of Mandy Wilson. He was the prime suspect in the murders of Susan, Caroline and Sarah.

He had, in fact, been interviewed about these cases before he went on trial. But if the police were hoping for a confession, their hopes were soon dashed. Under questioning, Black spoke freely about the abduction of Mandy Wilson, his attraction to little girls, even his masturbatory practices. However, when it came to the abductions and murders of the three little girls, he clammed up.

Unable to obtain a confession, the police went back to their evidence and began building a case against Black. Unfortunately, there was no forensic evidence to link him to any of the crimes, but there were work records, wage books, and credit cards receipts for fuel purposes. Following this trail, investigators were able to place Black in the vicinity of each crime on the days they occurred. They were also able to connect him to each dumpsite.

But they needed more. It came in the form of the failed abduction of a 15-year-old girl named Teresa Thornhill. Both Thornhill and her friend Andrew Beeson, who'd confronted the abductor and helped foil the attempt, were able to identify Black as the perpetrator.

By the end of 1990, the police had gathered a mountain of circumstantial evidence against Black. However, they were worried about bringing the matter to trial without forensics or a confession. They, therefore, re-interviewed Black, grilling him rigorously over three days. Still, the killer refused to admit to the murders. The police were going to have to go to trial with what they had.

Black's trial eventually got underway on 13 April 1994. He denied all of the charges, but the prosecution was able to build a compelling circumstantial case against him, placing him at each of the crime scenes and showing similarities between the three murders and the attempted abductions of Mandy Wilson and Teresa Thornhill.

On May 19, the jury found Black guilty on all counts. He was sentenced to life imprisonment, with the stipulation that he serve at least 35 years before he is eligible for parole. This would keep him behind bars until at least 2029, when he will be 82-years-old.

He continues to be a suspect in at least nine other abduction murders, bearing his familiar M.O.

# William Palmer

*The Rugeley Poisoner*

The case of William Palmer is one of the most notorious in British legal history. Born in the town of Rugeley, Staffordshire, on August 6, 1824, Palmer took to crime at an early age. By the time he was 17, he had already been accused of a number of offenses, ranging from embezzlement to running an abortion service. He was also suspected of poisoning a drinking companion, and although nothing could be proven, he was dismissed from his medical internship.

Overcoming these setbacks, Palmer qualified as a doctor from St Bartholomew's Hospital in 1846. Thereafter he settled down to a modest practice in his hometown and in 1847 wed Ann Thornton at St. Nicholas Church, Abbots Bromley. Their first son, William Brookes Palmer, was born a year later, in 1848.

From the outside, Palmer appeared to be living the life of a respectable small town doctor. The truth was somewhat different. Local gossip had it that Palmer had several mistresses, including some of his servant girls. He also had a serious gambling problem and was deeply in hock due to money lost on card games and horse racing.

The first of several suspicious deaths connected to Palmer occurred on January 18, 1849, when his mother-in-law, Ann Mary Thornton, died suddenly while visiting the Palmer household. Mrs. Thornton was only 50 years old at the time and in good health, yet her death seems to have aroused no suspicion. Palmer's wife inherited a considerable sum from the estate.

Sixteen months later, on May 10, 1850, another houseguest of the Palmers, Leonard Bladen, died. And over the next four years, the household appeared cursed as four of the Palmer children died in infancy.

There were other suspicious deaths, too. Joseph Bentley, an elderly uncle of Palmer, died on October 27, 1852, his passing attracting no attention from the authorities. Not even the death of Palmer's wife Ann, just 27 years old when she suddenly became ill and died, aroused much suspicion. Palmer was carrying on an affair with one of his maids at the time. She later bore him an illegitimate son. The child, like so many of Palmer's offspring, did not survive infancy.

Palmer had taken out a life insurance policy on his wife, and her death brought him the considerable sum of £13, 000. But even that was not enough to service his gambling debt. He needed more money, and soon turned his deadly attentions to his brother. Walter Palmer was insured for £10,000 and died on August 16, 1855. However, the insurance company refused to pay out, claiming that not enough time had elapsed since the purchase of the policy. And there was a further setback for Palmer when one of his former lovers, the daughter of a Staffordshire police officer, began blackmailing him.

Heavily in debt, Palmer set off for the Shrewsbury Horse Races on November 13, 1855. However, if he was hoping for a change of luck, it did not materialize. He lost heavily over the three days of the meeting.

Palmer's companion at the races, John Parsons Cook, had considerably better luck and invited Palmer for a celebratory drink at a pub called "The Raven." Palmer reciprocated by inviting Cook to dinner at his house on November 17. Immediately after, Cook began complaining of feeling ill. Within a short while, he was so poorly that Palmer insisted he stay until he had recovered. Ever the good friend, he even stated his commitment to personally nurse Cook back to health.

The next day, a housemaid at the Palmer residence sampled a broth that Palmer had prepared for Cook. A short while later she was violently ill. Palmer meanwhile, had departed for London, to collect the money Cook had won at the races. He was back on November 19. On November 21, John Cook was dead.

Cook's stepfather, a Mr. Stevens, was the executor of his estate and was immediately suspicious of the circumstances surrounding his stepson's death. He called for an autopsy, the examination completed on November 26. A coroner's inquest was held in early December and delivered a unanimous verdict of "death by willful murder."

The obvious suspect was William Palmer. Yet there was very little evidence to connect him with the crime. Indeed, Palmer would likely have gotten away with it, had he not tried to bribe several people involved with the inquest. That aroused suspicion, and when it was learned that Palmer had bought a quantity of strychnine just before Cook's death, he was placed under arrest.

Shortly after Palmer was detained, the bodies of his wife and brother were exhumed. However, there was not enough evidence to charge Palmer with murder in their deaths. Not that the prosecution needed it. They believed that they had a strong enough case against Palmer for the murder of John Cook.

Palmer went on trial at London's Old Bailey in May 1856, the trial having been moved due to the ill feeling towards him in his native Staffordshire. The evidence was largely circumstantial, but it was enough for the jury to find him guilty of murder. (Many modern legal scholars believe that the evidence was not enough to convict him.)

Palmer went to the gallows outside Stafford Prison on June 14, 1856, watched by a raucous crowd of some 30,000. As he stepped onto the platform, Palmer is said to have examined the trapdoor and remarked to the executioner, "Are you sure it's safe?"

# Burke and Hare

*The Body Snatchers*

Dr. Robert Knox had served under Wellington at Waterloo and had seen his fair share of horrendous, battlefield injuries. It had equipped him with a unique perspective on human anatomy, so that when he set up shop as an extramural lecturer in Edinburgh in the 1820's his anatomy classes were among the best attended in the city.

The problem for Dr. Knox, as for all of his profession during that time, was acquiring enough cadavers to meet the growing demand. British law stipulated that only the bodies of executed criminals could be used for dissection, and while that had been adequate in earlier decades, a number of converging influences made it less so now. For a start, there was the burgeoning interest in the medical sciences, with students flocking from far and wide to attend classes. Then there were the more lenient laws of a new, enlightened age, resulting in fewer executions and thus, fewer legally available cadavers.

It all added up to a massive headache for the medical establishment, but there was a way, illicit admittedly, of circumventing the problem. The demand for human corpses had created an opportunity for an entirely new sub-class of criminal. These ghouls (known colloquially as 'Body Snatchers' or 'Resurrection Men') made their living by trading in the dead. They'd haunt graveyards by night, disinterring freshly buried corpses and carrying them off to be sold to some desperate anatomist. This activity was, of course, illegal and the risks were great. But it paid well, and there was no shortage of takers.

Contrary to what is often written about them, William Burke and William Hare did not start out as body snatchers. In fact, it would be fair to say that Burke and Hare never disturbed a crypt in their lives. Their approach was more pragmatic, less labor intensive. Rather than digging up corpses, they simply created them.

William Burke was born in the parish of Urney, County Tyrone, in what is now Northern Ireland. As a young man, he tried his hand at various trades before joining the army, where he served in the Donegal Militia as an officer's servant. He was married at Ballinha, County Mayo, while still in the military. After being discharged, Burke decided to move to Scotland to work on the Union Canal. His wife would not accompany him, and so he deserted her and their two children.

While working on the canal, Burke lived in Maddiston where he met Helen McDougal, a native Scot who was then living with a man with whom she had two children. Burke and McDougal left Maddiston together after the canal was completed, apparently leaving the two children behind. They traveled to Peebles and Leith and then to Edinburgh, scraping a living by working as farm laborers, selling old clothes, and mending shoes.

William Hare had also come from Ireland to Scotland to work on the Union Canal, although whether he ever encountered Burke there is unknown. After the completion of the canal, he moved to the West Port area of Edinburgh, where he found cheap lodgings at the boarding house of a man named Logue and his wife Margaret, also an Irish native. When Logue died in 1826, Hare moved in with Margaret and they ran the lodging house as man and wife.

When Burke and McDougal arrived in Edinburgh, they too, took up residence in West Port and after encountering Margaret (whom Burke knew), they moved in as paying lodgers of the Hares. The four of them became close companions, although they quarreled often and, when the drink was flowing, sometimes exchanged blows.

In November 1827, one of Hare's lodgers, an army pensioner named Donald, became ill and died. Hare was angered by the man's death as Donald had passed away owing £4 in rent. He soon struck upon a plan to recoup his loss. With Burke's assistance, he removed Donald's body from its coffin, replacing it with an equal weight of tree bark. He then hid the corpse until the coffin was collected, whereupon he and Burke went off to find the classroom of anatomy instructor Professor Monro. Asking for directions, they were directed instead to the Surgeons' Square premises of Professor Robert Knox. Knox's assistant met Burke and Hare at the door, told them that he would be interested in buying the body, and instructed them to deliver it after nightfall.

That night Burke and Hare returned carrying a large sack. They were hustled inside, and after examining the body Knox's assistant offered £7.10s for it. The two men quickly agreed. They left the doctor's rooms buzzing with excitement. Not only had Hare recovered his arrear rent, they'd actually realized a profit from the transaction. It was the easiest money they'd ever made. Back at the boarding house, drunk on whiskey from their ill-gotten gains, they wondered if they'd stumbled on a way of making a considerable amount of money for very little work.

Their chance of another windfall came soon after. Another of Hare's lodgers, Joseph, fell ill not many days after Donald's demise. Joseph was not in debt to Hare and was not nearly as ill as Donald had been, but Burke and Hare decided that he was probably in pain and that he was more than likely going to die anyway. They resolved to put the old man out of his misery. After plying Joseph with whiskey until he passed out, one of the men pinned him down, while the other placed a hand over his nose and mouth, suffocating him. It was all over in minutes and Joseph was transported to Dr. Knox's door that very night, earning his murderers a £10 fee.

The killers now had a simple and effective method figured out, one that left no marks on the body and gave the impression that the individual had died of natural causes. However, their potential pool of victims was limited. None of the other lodgers appeared in any way unwell. Burke and Hare decided that if they were going to make a business of this, they were going to have to spread their net wider.

In February 1828, an elderly woman named Abigail Simpson made her monthly sojourn into Edinburgh to collect her pension money. As she was about to begin her return journey to the village of Gilmerton, she encountered William Hare, who invited her back to his boarding house to rest up and have a drink. Abigail agreed and soon Hare, along with Burke and their female accomplices were plying the old woman with liquor. Eventually, she passed out, but whatever plans Burke and Hare had for her would have to wait. They were too drunk themselves, to carry through.

The following morning, Abigail woke with a hangover and accepted Hare's remedy of another whiskey. Several glasses later and she was again unconscious. She put up no resistance as Burke and Hare smothered her. She was packed into a tea chest and taken that evening to Knox's rooms.

Burke and Hare walked away with another £10 in their pockets, a considerable sum in those days but one that was quickly blown on liquor. Soon they were casting around for another victim, and one presented itself in the form of another of Hare's lodgers. The Englishman, who sold matches for a living, developed a mild case of influenza. Burke and Hare charitably put the poor fellow out of his suffering.

Although Hare and Burke have gone down in history as the perpetrators of these dreadful crimes, the roles played by

Margaret and Helen should not be understated. One day Margaret Hare encountered an old woman on the streets of Edinburgh and invited her back to the house where she began plying her with drink. Once the woman passed out, Margaret sent for her husband to complete the task. Another unnamed woman was similarly lured and dispatched, this time by Burke.

On the morning of April 9, 1828, Burke encountered two 18-year-old prostitutes, Mary Paterson and Janet Brown, drinking in a tavern in Canongate. He invited them to breakfast at his brother's house in Gibb's Close, where they continued drinking until Mary eventually passed out. Burke and Janet then left for another tavern, but on their return, they were confronted by a furious Helen McDougal.

A fight ensued between Burke and Helen, and Janet decided to leave, saying she would return later to fetch Mary, who'd continued sleeping through the entire incident. However, by the time Janet did return, Mary was gone. Burke insisted that she'd left of her own accord, but Mary was never seen again.

The murder of Mary Paterson was the riskiest Burke and Hare had yet committed. Not only had she been seen with Burke prior to her death, but when she was laid out for Dr. Knox's anatomy class, several of the students recognized her. Nonetheless, no one was concerned enough to go to the authorities, even though Janet would continue to walk the streets of Edinburgh for a long time inquiring about her friend's whereabouts.

Burke and Hare, meanwhile, were already looking for their next victim. They found her in a beggar-woman named Effie who Burke occasionally bought scraps of leather from, in his legitimate trade as a cobbler. One morning, after transacting some business with Effie, Burke invited her back to the lodging house for a drink. Once she passed out, he and Hare suffocated her, collecting their £10 for the corpse later that evening.

It was all becoming too easy for Burke and Hare and they became bolder in their pursuit of saleable "stock." With the next victim, Burke took an audacious risk. Seeing two policemen escorting an obviously inebriated woman to the lockup, he intervened, told them that he knew her and offered to escort her home. The officers handed the woman over and she was soon on her way to Surgeons' Square for another £10 payout.

In June 1828, Burke was stopped by an old woman and her mute, 12-year-old grandson. The woman asked him for directions and Burke said that he would be happy to take them to where they needed to go, but suggested that they stop at his house to rest first. The woman, who was a stranger to Edinburgh, gladly agreed. Once at the boarding house, she was plied with alcohol and was soon inebriated. Burke and Hare then murdered her by their usual method. They then discussed what to do with the boy, who was with Margaret and Helen in another room. Eventually, it was decided that Hare would do away with the boy. Stretching the child over his knee, he proceeded to break the boy's back. He would later say that this was the murder that disturbed him the most, as he was haunted by the expression in the boy's eyes. Nonetheless, the bodies were forced into a herring barrel and conveyed to Surgeons' Square, where they fetched £8 each.

Not long after the double murder, Burke and Helen McDougal left Edinburgh for a short while to visit some of Helen's relatives.

When they returned, they moved out of Hare's lodging house and into quarters nearby. Burke would later say that this was because Margaret had suggested that they should murder Helen, and also because he'd learned that Hare had been working solo in supplying Dr. Knox during his absence.

Whatever their differences, the two men continued to work as a team. A visitor to Burke's new boarding house, named Mrs. Hostler, disappeared and was never seen again. Then a relative of Helen's, Ann McDougal, came to visit Edinburgh from Falkirk and disappeared.

The next victim was Mary Haldane, an elderly prostitute, down on her luck, who Hare allowed to sleep in his stables. A few days later, Mary's daughter Peggy arrived to enquire about her mother's whereabouts. Margaret and Helen both heatedly denied that Mary had been there, while Hare admitted that she had but had later moved on. Hare then offered Peggy a drink and then another. Before long she'd joined her mother at Dr. Knox's surgery.

Mary Haldane had been well known in the neighborhood and her disappearance caused a stir. However, Burke and Hare were by now brimming with confidence at their ability to get away with murder. The next victim was almost their undoing.

James Wilson, known locally as Daft Jamie, was a character around West Port. The 18-year-old was mentally retarded and walked with a limp, but was loved by everyone for his high spirits.

In early October 1828, Hare came across Jamie wandering the streets, looking for his mother. Hare said that he knew where she was and invited Jamie to wait for her at the boarding house. The moment Hare had him indoors, Margaret ran to fetch Burke from a nearby tavern. Hare tried to convince Jamie to have some whiskey, but Jamie drank only a sip and refused more. Nonetheless, he was soon asleep on a spare bed. Burke and Hare then attempted to suffocate him, but Jamie fought furiously, getting the upper hand on Burke before Hare jumped in to help and together they overpowered him.

That evening, the Burke and Hare collected £10 for Jamie's body, but soon questions were being asked about his disappearance. When the body was uncovered during Dr. Knox's anatomy class, several students recognized Jamie's face and the well-known deformity of his foot. However, Dr. Knox denied that the body was Jamie, and began the dissection quickly, rendering the corpse unrecognizable.

On Halloween morning, Burke was drinking at a local tavern when an old woman entered. Noticing that she had an Irish accent, and hearing that she was Mary Docherty from Innisowen, Burke struck up a conversation, saying that his mother was a Docherty from Innisowen, and that they must be related. He then invited Mary back to his house. Also staying at the boarding house was a couple, James and Ann Gray.

After a few drinks, Burke convinced Docherty to stay overnight with him and Helen, while the Grays were sent to spend the evening at the Hare's lodging house. Later that night, an upstairs neighbor claimed to have heard a woman's voice calling out "Murder!" from Burke and Helen's rooms.

The following morning, the Grays returned and found Mary Docherty was gone. They asked about her and Helen told them that she'd thrown the old lady out after she became overly friendly with Burke. Later, when Ann Gray wanted to fetch some stockings she'd left behind in a spare room, Helen shouted at her to stay out.

Later that day, the Grays found themselves alone in the house for a short while. Ann Gray, who was suspicious about being barred from the spare room, decided to take a look and was horrified to find Mary Docherty's body concealed under the bed. The Grays ran from the house but encountered Helen on the way out. James Gray demanded to know what Helen knew about the body, and Helen then begged them not to say anything, offering £10 a week for their silence. The couple refused and went to fetch a policeman.

By the time the police arrived, Burke and McDougal were nowhere to be found and a neighbor told the officers that two men had recently left the house carrying a tea chest. Burke and Helen returned home soon after and asked innocently what was going on. The police then separated them and asked them individually, what had become of Mrs. Docherty. Burke and McDougal told the same story. The old woman had left their home at seven o'clock. However, Burke said it was seven in that morning while, according to Helen, it was seven in the evening.

The discrepancy was suspicious enough for Burke and McDougal to be taken in for questioning. Then, an anonymous tip led the police to Dr. Knox's surgery, where Docherty's body was discovered. Soon William and Margaret Hare were also in custody and the police began to discover the dreadful truth about the disappearances of 16 people from West Port during the previous eleven months.

However, the case against Burke and Hare was far from solid. There were no eyewitnesses to any of the killings and, while the authorities did have the body of Mary Docherty, they couldn't say for sure how she'd died. The possibility also existed that the two would blame each other, leaving it impossible for the jury to decide which one was actually responsible for the murders. Faced with allowing one, or both, of the murderers the chance to walk free, the Lord Advocate opted for the latter. With the assumption that William Burke, the more intelligent of the two, was the leader, an offer was made to Hare – testify against Burke and McDougal in exchange for immunity.

Hare readily agreed, and Burke and McDougal were both charged with the murder of Mary Docherty. Burke, in addition, was charged with the killings of Daft Jamie and Mary Paterson.

The trial began on Christmas Eve 1828 and concluded 24 hours later on Christmas morning. The jury deliberated for only fifty minutes before coming back with their verdicts - Burke was found guilty and Helen was freed by the uniquely Scottish 'Not Proven' verdict. Despite his own predicament, Burke reportedly embraced Helen at the verdict, saying, "You are out of the scrape!"

Burke was executed on January 28, 1829, his body thereafter given over for public dissection. Helen, on being released, went back to the house she had shared with Burke. But an angry mob found her and she would have likely been lynched were it not for the intervention of the police. She fled to England, but her notoriety followed her even there and she was driven out of Newcastle. No one knows for certain what became of her although one version of events has her moving to Australia and dying there in 1868.

Margaret Hare also disappeared. After her release, she had to be rescued from lynch mobs in Glasgow and Greenock. She is believed to have eventually gone back to Ireland.

William Hare was released in early February of 1829, but his fate, too, is unknown. A popular tale tells of his being blinded by a mob who threw him into a lime pit, and of ending up as a beggar on the streets of London.

Dr. Robert Knox was cleared of complicity in Burke and Hare's activities although the court of public opinion still deemed him guilty. He eventually left Edinburgh and moved to London where he held a post at the Cancer Hospital until his death in 1862.

# Bruce Peter George Lee

*"I am devoted to fire. Fire is my master." – Bruce Lee*

In common with most serial killers, Bruce Lee had an inauspicious start to life. His mother was a prostitute, and he came into the world with a number of birth defects including epilepsy and a congenital spastic disorder, which left him with a limp and a withered right arm. Until the age of three, he was raised by his grandmother. Later, his mother took responsibility for his upbringing, but he'd spend much of his youth in children's homes, where he suffered bullying and abuse as well as being introduced to homosexual sex. He left school at 16 and found work as a laborer. At 19, he changed his name from Peter George Dinsdale to Bruce Lee, in honor of his favorite martial arts actor.

By that time, Lee was already an obsessive pyromaniac, responsible for at least 23 deaths, the first of which occurred in

1973, when Lee was just 12 years old. On June 23 of that year, Lee set fired to the home of a pupil who attended the same school as him. Richard Ellerington, aged just six, died in the blaze.

Four months later, on October 12, 1973, Lee poured kerosene – his favorite accelerant – through the mailbox of a senile old man named Bernard Smythe. 72-year-old Smythe was trapped in the blaze and burned alive. Kerosene was detected at the scene but it was assumed that it was from a heater in the victim's home.

Two weeks after the Smythe murder, Lee struck again. The victim, this time, was David Brewer, aged 34. Brewer had recently suffered an accident at work and was at home recuperating when Lee snuck into his apartment. Finding the man asleep on a couch, he doused him with kerosene and set him alight. It would later emerge that Smythe had quarreled with Lee two days before his death.

The next to die was 82-year-old Elizabeth Rokahr, burned to death on the night of December 23, 1974. Her death was ruled accidental, the theory being that she'd fallen asleep while smoking in bed.

On July 3, 1976, a fire broke out at the home of the Andrews family. Three young children were in the house at the time, being supervised by their grandmother. The old woman was able to rescue two of the children, but one-year-old Andrew Edwards succumbed to the flames. The grandmother was so traumatized by the incident that she'd end up being confined to a mental institution. Lee would later admit to setting the blaze.

Lee's next victim was even younger than Andrew Edwards. Katrina Thacker was just six months old when she died in a fire at her home. Lee was an acquaintance of the Thacker family but had recently argued with them over his habit of arriving uninvited at their home. An inquest ruled that the blaze had been caused by a stray spark from the fireplace, even though Mrs. Thacker insisted that no fire had been lit that day.

On January 5, 1977, Lee committed his worst atrocity yet, setting fire to the Wensley Lodge retirement home and causing the deaths of 11 elderly men, ranging in age from 65 to 95. The fire was blamed on plumbing work done earlier in the day, where workmen had used a blowtorch. Lee would later confess to starting the blaze.

On April 27, 1977, Lee started a fire at another family home, killing a mentally handicapped girl of 13 named Deborah Hooper, and seven-year-old Mark Jordan, a friend of the family, who was staying the night. On January 6, Lee killed 24-year-old Christine Dickson and three of her young sons, Mark, 5, Steven, 4, and Michael, 16 months. Mrs. Dickson made it out of the burning house with her baby, then handed him over to a neighbor and ran back in a vain effort to save the other boys. The police surmised that Mark and Steven had started the fire while playing with matches.

Thus far, all of Lee's crimes had been put down to accidents. However, in the next incident, there was little doubt that an arsonist was responsible.

On December 4, 1979, a fire broke out at the Hastie home in Hull, East Yorkshire. Charles Hastie, 15, and his younger brothers Paul, 12, and Peter, 8, were all asleep in the house when the fire happened. Also in the home were the boys' mother, Edith, as well as another brother, Thomas. The boys' father was serving a prison term at the time, while their three sisters were spending the night with relatives.

Charles Hastie was the first to wake. Noticing smoke in his room, he rushed to wake his siblings, then ran to his mother's room as the fire took hold. Pushing Edith from an upstairs window, he returned to the bedroom he shared with Peter and Paul. There, all three of them were overcome by the flames. Charles died the next day, having suffered severe burns. Peter and Paul were rushed to the burns unit at Pinderfields Hospital in Wakefield but succumbed within the week. Their mother survived, as did younger brother Thomas.

The presence of spilled kerosene on the front porch made it obvious that the fire had been deliberately set and the subsequent investigation turned up no shortage of potential arsonists. The Hastie family, it appeared, had made many enemies in the neighborhood, due to their involvement in petty crime, bullying and several vendettas. The police, therefore, focused their attention on people who might bear a grudge against the family. One of those questioned was Bruce Lee.

Lee admitted to knowing Charles Hastie but insisted that he was not involved in setting the fire. With no evidence to suggest otherwise, the police released him.

Then, a new angle emerged. It appeared that Charles Hastie had been moonlighting as a homosexual hustler, servicing his clients in public restrooms near his home. Following this line of investigation, 18,000 men were questioned. Once again, Bruce Lee was among them.

This time, he inexplicably decided to confess. He said that he and Charles Hastie had been involved in a homosexual relationship, but that Charles had begun blackmailing him, threatening to report him to the police for having sex with a minor. Lee didn't stop at the Hastie murders, though. As detectives listened gape-mouthed, he admitted to 23 murders over the last six years, all of which had previously been considered accidents. "I am devoted to fire," he said. "Fire is my master, and that is why I cause these fires."

Bruce Lee went on trial at Leeds Crown Court in January 1981, charged with 26 counts of murder. He denied the charges but entered guilty pleas instead to manslaughter. The pleas were accepted and he was ordered to be detained indefinitely under the Mental Health Act. He is currently an inmate at Rampton Secure Hospital.

# Harold Shipman

## Dr. Death

*"He was exercising the ultimate power of controlling life and death, and repeated the act so often he must have found the drama of taking life to his taste."* – Richard Henriques, prosecutor at Shipman's trial

Kathleen Grundy was a vivacious widow with energy to burn and a great love of life. The wealthy 81-year-old had once served as the mayor of Hyde, Lancashire. She was a loved and respected member of the community, noted for her charity work. One of Kathleen's causes was the Age Concern Club, where she helped serve meals to elderly pensioners. She was passionate about this work and known for her punctuality and reliability. So when she didn't show up on June 24, 1998, her friends were immediately concerned. A few of them set off for Kathleen's home, where they found her lying on the sofa, fully dressed. When they'd last seen her, she'd been her usual chirpy self. Now, she was dead.

Kathleen Grundy had been a patient of Dr. Harold Shipman, who had, in fact, visited her just a few hours before her death. Mrs. Grundy's friends placed a call to Dr. Shipman and he arrived soon after and pronounced her dead.

A short while later, Mrs. Grundy's daughter, Angela Woodruff, got a call from the police, informing her of her mother's death. Angela was stunned. As far as she knew, her mother had been in very good health, despite her advanced age. Angela immediately phoned Dr. Shipman for an explanation. The doctor was out, but he later phoned back and told Angela that her mother had died of old age. He was also at pains to stress that a postmortem was unnecessary because he had seen her shortly before her death. Lastly, he recommended to Angela that she should have her mother cremated.

Angela Woodruff ignored this last piece of advice and in keeping with her mother's wishes had her buried. Then, following the funeral, she received a disconcerting call from a firm of solicitors. They claimed to be holding a copy of Mrs. Grundy's last will and testament.

A solicitor herself, Angela had always handled her mother's legal affairs and as far as she knew her firm held the original document. She therefore set up a meeting to view the new will. The moment she saw the poorly worded, poorly typed document, she knew that it was a fake. "My mother was a meticulously tidy person," she later testified, "the thought of her signing a document which is so badly typed didn't make any sense."

But the shoddy composition of the document was not the only concern. The new will bequeathed all of Kathleen Grundy's worldly possessions to her physician, Dr. Harold Shipman. Angela knew that her mother had liked and respected Shipman, but she could not understand why she'd have left her entire estate to him. She began to suspect that someone had drawn up the document in order to frame the doctor for Kathleen's death. However, after interviewing the two witnesses to the will, she reluctantly came to the conclusion that Dr. Shipman had murdered her mother for money. It was then that she took her suspicions to the police.

The case landed on the desk of Detective Superintendent Bernard Postles, and he quickly drew the same conclusion as Angela Woodruff. The will was quite obviously a forgery, and a crude one at that. It cast suspicion on the doctor, especially since Mrs. Grundy had died so soon after bequeathing her estate to him.

However, in order to prove murder, a postmortem would have to be carried out. An exhumation order was therefore obtained and hair and tissue samples were taken from the deceased and sent to different labs for analysis.

The police, meanwhile, were concerned that Dr. Shipman might hear of the exhumation and be scared into destroying evidence. They therefore launched a raid on the doctor's home and offices, logging into evidence a number of medical documents and an old typewriter, which would later prove to have been used to type the fake will.

Then the toxicology report arrived, and the police were in for a shock. They had expected that the doctor, with his medical knowledge, would have used a poison that would be difficult to trace - insulin, perhaps, which the body produces naturally. Instead, Shipman had injected Mrs. Grundy with a massive dose of morphine, one of the easiest toxins to detect. It pointed to someone confident in his ability to avoid detection, someone perhaps, who'd gotten away with this sort of thing before. Postles began to fear that Kathleen Grundy was not Dr. Shipman's only victim. He'd soon be proven devastatingly correct in that assumption.

Harold Frederick Shipman was born in Nottingham on January 14, 1946, the middle of three children. His mother, Vera, doted on him and kept a very strict rein on who Freddy (as he was affectionately called) was allowed to associate with. As a young boy, he did exceptionally well at school, although as he grew older his academic performance dropped off somewhat. In 1963, when he was 17 years old, Shipman's beloved mother died of lung cancer. She was only 43 at the time, and Shipman nursed her through her final months.

In 1965, Shipman went to study medicine at Leeds University, graduating in 1970. He then served an internship at Pontefract General Infirmary before entering work as a GP at a practice in Todmorden. By now, Shipman was already married and the father of two young children. He also proved to be an excellent GP, respected and well liked by staff and patients. Yet there was another side to Shipman. He could be confrontational, combative and rude. At times, he humiliated people and was fond of referring to those who disagreed with him as "stupid." He also insisted on having things done his way, even overruling the more experienced doctors in the practice.

Shipman had only been at Todmorden for two years when his career came to an abrupt halt. He began suffering blackouts, which he self-diagnosed as epilepsy. The truth was rather more sinister. Shipman had become addicted to the morphine-like drug pethidine and had been making out fraudulent prescriptions to obtain his fix. When this was discovered, he was fired from his job and charged with fraud and forgery. The penalty was ridiculously lenient – a £600 fine.

Although the General Medical Council did not see fit to strike him off, Shipman was barred from working in any capacity that gave him access to drugs. When this censure expired in 1977, he re-emerged as a GP in Hyde.

As he had at Todmorden, Shipman quickly established himself as a valuable member of staff. His new colleagues at the Donnybrook Surgery respected his work, while the patients loved his friendly bedside manner, even if he could be arrogant and patronizing at times. In 1992, he split from the Donnybrook practice to set up on his own, just around the corner on Market Street. He took with him a large list of patients.

Over the next five years, Shipman built up a steady practice of loyal patients, many of them elderly. However, by 1997, the first suspicions had begun to emerge about Shipman. The staff at Massey's, a local funeral parlor, had begun to notice similarities in many of the deceased that were sent to them for burial. Although all were elderly women, most of them were known to have been in good health immediately prior to their deaths. All had lived alone and all were found fully dressed, sitting in a chair or lying on a couch. If that wasn't enough of a coincidence, all had either been found dead by Dr. Shipman or had been visited by him shortly before they died.

At the same time, doctors at the Brooke Surgery, just over the road from Shipman, were becoming concerned about the number of deaths at his practice. Both they and the directors of Massey's passed on their concerns to the authorities. However, a covert examination of Shipman's records found no evidence of wrongdoing, and the authorities declined to take the matter further.

Now, though, the police had every reason to investigate. Before long, fifteen bodies had been exhumed and Shipman found himself charged with multiple counts of murder.

The sheer scale of Shipman's killing spree is astonishing. The first murder was believed to have occurred on March 6, 1995, when Shipman injected Marie West with diamorphine. He attributed her death to a stroke.

Sixteen months later, on July 11, 1996, Shipman visited Irene Turner at her home. Mrs. Turner had recently returned from a holiday and had a cold, for which Shipman administered an injection. The syringe contained morphine and Mrs. Turner died soon after. He listed cause of death as diabetes.

On February 28, 1997, a friend of 77-year-old Lizzie Adams arrived for a visit and found Shipman at Ms. Adams' home and her friend sprawled out on the couch. Shipman claimed that he'd found Ms. Adams in this condition and had just called an ambulance. Then he pretended to make another call canceling the ambulance, saying that the patient had died. Phone records show that neither call was actually made. Shipman recorded cause of death as pneumonia.

On April 25, 1997, Shipman called on Jean Lilley. When a neighbor saw him leave she went to check on her friend and found her dead. Shipman claimed that the 59-year-old had died of heart failure, but a pathologist later found cause of death to be morphine poisoning.

The next to die was 63-year-old Ivy Lomas, killed at Shipman's surgery on May 29, 1997. Two days later, Shipman altered her medical records to fit in with his diagnosis. Mrs. Lomas was a regular at his surgery and Shipman often referred to her as a nuisance when talking to his staff.

Muriel Grimshaw was found dead at her home on July 14, 1997. Shipman claimed she'd died of a stroke, caused by hypertension. He then altered her medical records to support his diagnosis.

On November 28, 1997, Shipman killed Marie Quinn with an injection of morphine. He claimed that Mrs. Quinn had called him saying that she'd just suffered a stroke. He'd rushed to her home, but she was dead when he arrived. Phone records show no calls by Mrs. Quinn to Shipman's surgery on the day in question.

Shipman's next victim was Kathleen Wagstaff, who he claimed had summoned him to her home on December 9, 1997. Records show that no such call was made. He said she died of heart disease, but no evidence was found of any such illness.

Bianka Pomfret died at her home on December 10, 1997, shortly after a visit from Shipman. He claimed she had died of coronary thrombosis. Forensic experts later found that Shipman had altered the patient's medical records in order to create a backdated history of heart problems.

Norah Nuttall was visited by Shipman on January 26, 1998. Less than an hour later, her son arrived to find his mother dead in a chair. Shipman said he had called an ambulance, then canceled it when he realized that Mrs. Nuttall was dead. Phone records showed that neither call was made.

Pamela Hillier, an active 68-year-old, was found dead on February 9, 1998. Shipman said she'd died of a massive stroke. It was later proven that he'd made ten changes to her medical records in order to support his diagnosis.

Maureen Ward, 57, had been suffering from cancer but was in remission at the time of her death on February 18, 1998. Shipman recorded her cause of death as a brain tumor, then altered her medical records to suggest that the cancer had spread to her brain.

A cancer specialist testified at trial that this was not the case and that Mrs. Ward had died from a massive overdose of diamorphine.

Winifred Mellor, 73, was found dead on May 11, 1998, having been visited by Shipman earlier in the day. He claimed she had died of coronary thrombosis and altered her medical records to make it look like she had been complaining of chest pains.

Joan Melia, 73, visited Shipman's surgery on June 12, 1998, suffering from a chest infection. Later that same day, he called at her home and claims to have found her dead. He issued a death certificate citing pneumonia aggravated by emphysema. A pathologist later found evidence of morphine but no serious lung problems.

And then there was Kathleen Grundy. Shipman had visited her early on the day of her death to take a blood sample, ostensibly for a study on aging. Unlike in the other murders, Shipman tried to profit from the crime with his falsified will. It was to prove his undoing.

Harold Shipman went on trial at the Preston Crown Court on October 5, 1999. The evidence against him was overwhelming and throughout the trial, he was caught in several lies. Yet he maintained his innocence to the end, offering up any number of ludicrous explanations for his actions.

The jury wasn't convinced. On the 31st January 2000, after six days of deliberation, they found Shipman guilty of fifteen counts of murder and one of forgery. He was sentenced to fifteen consecutive life terms, with the recommendation that he should never be released.

Harold Shipman, Britain's most prolific serial killer, was behind bars. Yet two questions remained: How many did Shipman kill, and why did he do it?

The answers will likely never be known. However, a public inquiry, chaired by High Court Judge, Dame Janet Smith, put the number of victims at 215 (171 women and 44 men, ranging in age from 41 to 93). Another investigation, conducted by University of Leicester professor Richard Baker, determined that Shipman killed at least 236 of his patients. Either of those numbers makes Shipman the most prolific serial killer in history.

As to why he did it, many contradictory theories have been suggested. Some psychoanalysts speculate that he hated older women; others feel he was re-creating his mother's death in order to satisfy some deep masochistic need. Still, others suggest that he considered himself superior to other people and believed he could do whatever he wanted without fear of discovery. Another theory is that he was fighting a compulsion he simply could not control and that the poorly forged will indicates he desperately wanted to be caught.

An element of truth probably exists in each of these explanations, but perhaps prosecutor Richard Henriques got closest to the answer when he said:

"He was exercising the ultimate power of controlling life and death, and repeated the act so often he must have found the drama of taking life to his taste."

We shall never know the whole truth. At around 6 a.m. on Tuesday, January 13, 2004, Harold Shipman was found hanging in his cell at Wakefield prison. He'd committed suicide by fashioning a noose from a bed sheet.

# Jack the Stripper

Duke's Meadows, on the banks of the River Thames in Chiswick, West London, was well known to the police as a spot favored by prostitutes for servicing their clients. It was called locally by the crude nickname, "Gobbler's Gulch," and the constables who routinely patrolled the area were quite used to finding the paths littered with discarded prophylactics. But, on the early morning of June 17, 1959, a somewhat more shocking discovery awaited them. A woman sat propped up against a small willow tree, her dress torn open to expose her breasts and the scratches on her throat. She had been strangled.

The victim was identified as Elizabeth Figg, a prostitute who also used the street name, Ann Phillips. Initial enquiries ruled out her pimp boyfriend, a Trinidadian boxer named Fenton "Baby" Ward, and the investigation pretty much ground to a halt after that. Even in that relatively non-violent era, prostitute murders were not uncommon. Elizabeth Figg was soon forgotten. It would be four years before anyone would have cause to mention her name again.

Gwynneth Rees had a lot in common with Elizabeth Figg. Like Figg, she'd come to London in her teens, looking for a more glamorous existence than her small hometown in South Wales offered. Like Figg, she soon drifted into the twilight world of prostitution. Like Figg, she ended up dead, her strangled body discovered on a garbage dump alongside the Thames on November 8, 1963. Rees had last been seen getting into a car with a man on September 29. A post-mortem would reveal that she'd been strangled with a ligature and that several of her teeth had been knocked out. She also had a sexually transmitted disease, an occupational hazard for 'working girls' in an era when many clients refused to wear condoms.

As the police looked into Gwynneth Rees' background, they found no shortage of suspects, chief among them her pimp, Cornelius "Connie" Whitehead. A violent criminal with links to the notorious Kray Twins, Whitehead was known to deliver savage beatings to his girls. Rees had recently run away from him and he was known to be looking for her.

Another theory was that Rees might have died as the result of an illegal abortion, but that didn't tally with the evidence. Presuming that the abortionist had to dispose of her body, why leave it where it was sure to be discovered? And why strangle her? Before long, the Rees case, like the Figg case before it, had gone cold. The public had very little interest in a couple of murdered prostitutes, and the police, therefore, had very little incentive for prioritizing the case.

But then another prostitute turned up dead.

Hanna Tailford was from a mining town in the Northeast of England. As a child, she was known for her disruptive behavior and had been expelled from several schools. As a teenager, she ran away to London, where she was soon involved in prostitution, with a sideline in petty theft.

On February 2, 1964, rowers on the Thames found Tailford's naked body floating in the river near Hammersmith Bridge. She'd been strangled and several of her teeth were missing. Her semen-stained panties had been stuffed into her mouth. Hannah Tailford was 30-years-old at the time of her death and had been working as a prostitute for over a decade. It was an ugly end to a joyless existence.

Although the Tailford murder bore obvious similarities to the Figg and Rees cases, the police had not yet flagged it as a series. Instead, their investigation focused on the sordid world that Hannah Tailford inhabited, a world of pornography and society sex parties. Tailford was known to have appeared in underground "stag films." She was also fond of sharing stories about the bizarre orgies she'd been paid to participate in. On one occasion she'd attended an orgy at the home of a French diplomat, on another, she'd been paid £25 to have sex with a man in a gorilla costume, while a crowd of upper-crust revelers cheered them on.

Might Tailford have been silenced by someone with connections to this sleazy world? The police seemed to think so. They interviewed hundreds of people who they knew to have used the services of prostitutes, among them an England international soccer player, and several clergymen.

The newspapers had another theory. They speculated that Tailford had fallen victim to a "homicidal maniac." Soon that premise would begin to gain traction.

On April 8, 1964, another naked body was fished from the Thames. She was Irene Lockwood, a 26-year-old prostitute, who'd last been seen alive in Chiswick the previous evening. She had been strangled with a ligature, probably fashioned from her own clothing.

The police soon discovered a number of reasons why someone might have wanted Irene Lockwood dead. A year earlier, Lockwood's close friend, Vicki Pender, had been found battered to death in her North London flat. Pender was found to have been involved in trying to blackmail her clients with photographs she'd taken of them, and Lockwood did not appear averse to similar scams. In fact, she was known to run a ruse where she'd ask her client to leave his clothes outside of the bedroom. Then, while she and the client had sex, an accomplice would emerge from hiding and go through the man's pockets, robbing him of cash and valuables.

As police continued their enquiries, another promising lead emerged. While searching Lockwood's apartment, they found a business card with the name "Kenny" on it, along with a telephone number. "Kenny" turned out to be Kenneth Archibald, a 57-year-old, former soldier and now caretaker at the Holland Park Tennis Club. Digging further the police discovered that Archibald ran an illegal late-night speakeasy from the caretaker's quarters at the club. Such illicit drinking clubs were common in London at the time, but Archibald offered his clientele more than just late night drinks. He also offered the services of ladies of the night, among them, Irene Lockwood.

Archibald was questioned by police and at first denied knowing Lockwood. However, after he was brought to Notting Hill police station for interrogation, he did an abrupt u-turn. Not only did he admit knowing Lockwood, he surprised officers by blurting, "I killed her. I have got to tell somebody about it."

He then went on to describe how he and Lockwood had gotten into an argument over money. "I must have lost my temper," he said, "I put my hands around her throat. I then proceeded to take her clothes off and rolled her into the river. I took her clothes home and burned them."

Archibald was arrested for the Lockwood murder, but senior investigators found it difficult to believe that this bumbling old man with the hearing aid, was the serial killer they sought. Within three days of Archibald's "confession" this belief was validated when a fifth naked body turned up in an alleyway in Brentford.

Helen Barthelemy, 22-years-old at the time of her death, had been strangled, and despite the location of the body, away from the river and a few miles from the others, police were in no doubt that it was part of the series. Like the other victims, Barthelemy was a streetwalker of slight stature who was suffering from an STD. She'd also acquired a police record for activities other than prostitution, having been arrested for luring a man to an isolated spot then robbing him with a straight razor. She had frequented many of the same pubs and speakeasies as Irene Lockwood and had possibly known her.

Other than the location in which Barthelemy's body was found there was one significant difference to the offers. The body was filthy, suggesting that it might have been stored somewhere before being dumped in the alley. There was also a promising clue, microscopic specks of different colored paint on her skin. Analysis of the paint revealed that it was the type used to spray cars and other metal work. From this, detectives concluded that the body might have been hidden in a building close to a spray-painting workshop, since this kind of paint can be carried on the air and can penetrate gaps in walls and doors.

While the police focused their attention in narrowing down the possible locations of such workshops, extra officers were assigned to patrol along the Thames. Such patrols had, in fact, been stepped up after the Lockwood murder. But no sooner had that trap been set than Helene Barthelemy's body was found away from the river. It was almost as though the killer knew what the police would do next.

Meanwhile, Commander George Hatherill, head of Scotland Yard's CID had assumed overall control of the case. On April 28, 1964, he took the unusual step of making a public appeal to prostitutes to come forward with information. Given their inherent distrust of the police, it may have been expected the appeal would fall on deaf ears. However, such was the level of fear among streetwalkers that within a couple of days, 45 women had come forward.

Another initiative that Hatherill put in place was the documenting of all license plate numbers of cars seen in areas frequented by prostitutes. A number of decoys were also set up in these areas, female officers dressed as hookers in an effort to flush out the killer.

Prostitutes, for their part, were not relying solely on the police for protection. Many armed themselves with knives in the hope of fending off an attack. 30-year-old Scot, Mary Fleming, a veteran of over 10 years on the streets, certainly carried one, and boasted to her colleagues about how she'd once fought off a client who tried to strangle her.

When her naked body was found in Chiswick in the early hours of June 14, 1964, there were signs that she had indeed put up a fight. In the end, though, it had done her no good. She'd been strangled, stripped and dumped. As in the case of Helen Barthelemy, tiny particles of industrial paint were found on the body.

The location of the dump site, on a residential street in an area where the police presence was heaviest, seemed to highlight the killer's arrogance. The prevailing view amongst the investigators was that this was not coincidental, but a deliberate attempt to make the police look stupid. They began to wonder whether that might not be the underlying motive behind the crimes.

Meanwhile, the press had dubbed the elusive killer as "Jack The Stripper," an obvious pun on the name of the most notorious serial killer of all time. "The Stripper" had already equaled the body count of his deadly namesake. The pressure was mounting on detectives to catch him before he killed again.

In July 1964, Kenneth Archibald went on trial for the murder of Irene Lockwood. He had since retracted his confession, claiming that he had been drunk and depressed when he'd made it. With no other evidence against him, he was acquitted. The investigators close to the case had never considered him a viable suspect anyway.

The summer of 1964 passed without further incident, but London's prostitute population continued to be on alert. Most still went around armed with knives, while many had taken to working in pairs for extra security. They may have believed that such measures would keep them safe from the Stripper. On October 23, they were proved wrong in that assumption.

Frances Brown was a 21-year-old hooker from Edinburgh. On the night of October 23, she was drinking in a Notting Hill pub with her friend, Kim Taylor. The two had teamed up to watch over each other and as they prepared to hit the streets for the evening, they joked about their chances of running into the killer. Later, they were approached by two punters and split up to get into separate cars.

When Brown failed to return, Taylor contacted the police, telling them that her friend got into either a Ford Zephyr or Zodiac. A month would pass before Frances Brown's body was found on a Kensington side street on November 25th. The killing bore all the hallmarks of Jack The Stripper; Brown was small in stature and was found stripped and strangled, with telltale paint spots on the body.

But at least the police now had an eyewitness description of the killer. Kim Taylor described a round-faced man of medium height and solid build. Psychologists suggested that he was likely to be a meek individual who deliberately sought out petite women, as they were easier to overpower.

By none of this got police any closer to catching the killer. By the beginning of 1965 they had interviewed thousands of people and examined hundreds of leads, and still The Stripper was at large. It was only a matter of time before he struck again.

On February 16, 1965, the naked body of a 28-year-old Irish hooker named Bridie O'Hara was found behind a storage shed on an industrial estate in Acton. This was less than a mile from where Mary Fleming had been dumped.

The news had barely hit the headlines when Scotland Yard announced a new lead investigator on the case. Detective Chief Superintendent John Du Rose had a phenomenal resolution record. Nicknamed "Four Day Johnny" for the speed with which he usually solved cases, he immediately doubled the number of officers working the case.

Every vehicle traveling around West London during the hours of darkness had its details logged, and any car found "curb crawling" for prostitutes was put on a special watch list. In addition, Du Rose stepped up the hunt for the site where the bodies had been kept. This search eventually paid off when a matching paint sample was found beneath a covered transformer on the Heron Trading Estate. It was just yards from where the body of Bridie O'Hara had been discovered. As the investigators had suspected, the premises faced a spray-painting workshop.

The killer's hideout had been found, but with over 7,000 people employed on the trading estate, the police still had a lot of work to do. They began simultaneously conducting interviews and matching license plate numbers against those they had on their lists. Soon they'd whittled that list down to three suspects and Du Rose confidently predicted that they'd soon have their man.

For whatever reason, the arrest never came. Clearly, Du Rose's optimism had been misplaced and the killer had escaped the police dragnet. But the operation had not been entirely a failure. There were no further murders after the killing of Bridie O'Hara.

Still, the question remains. Who was Jack the Stripper?

Five years after the last murder, in 1970, John Du Rose gave an interview to BBC television. In it, the by-now retired detective claimed that he knew the identity of Jack The Stripper. He said that his detectives had been preparing to make an arrest when the suspect had committed suicide, gassing himself in a lock-up garage in South West London.

In his 1971 biography, Murder Was My Business, Du Rose repeated his claim, saying that the police strategy had been to use the media to scare the man into giving himself up. Instead, the killer had taken his own life, leaving a note, which said that he was "unable to take the strain any longer." Du Rose failed to name the suspect, referring to him only as "Big John."

Author Brian McConnell (in his 1974 book on the case, Found Naked And Dead) names the same suspect, saying he was a respectable man in his 40s, with a wife and several children. He was born in Scotland and had had a tough upbringing, marred by physical abuse. While serving in World War Two, he began using prostitutes and was known to turn violent when he'd been drinking. After the war, he became a police officer, but he quit after he was turned down for promotion to detective. He found work as a security guard, but harbored a deep resentment towards the police force over its perceived rejection of him. Part of the motive for the crimes was to humiliate the police. John had been a security guard at the Heron Trading Estate at the time of the murders. He had committed suicide shortly after the Bridie O' Hara murder.

On the face of it, "Big John" looks like a viable suspect, and for years, the version of events put forward by Du Rose and McConnell was accepted as true. But in 1972, author David Seabrook began researching the case, for a book that would later be released as Jack Of Jumps. Granted unprecedented access to the original case files, Seabrook spent several years on painstaking research. His conclusion was to roundly reject Du Rose's suspect.

According to Seabrook, the man suspected by Du Rose was Mungo Ireland, a Scot living in Putney at the time of the murders. Ireland could not have been the killer, he says, because he was in Scotland at the time of the Bridie O'Hara murder. Furthermore, there was very little evidence to link Ireland to the murders. He worked at the Heron Trading Estate for a period of only three weeks and there are no links to any of the other crimes. Most notably his license plate number was never recorded in the areas the police had under surveillance.

Ireland was found dead in his car on 3 March 1965. His suicide note read:

*"I can't stick it any longer. It may be my fault but not all of it. I'm sorry Harry is a burden to you. Give my love to the kid.*

*Farewell,*

*Jock.*

*PS. To save you and the police looking for me I'll be in the garage."*

Much has been made of that last line. Why would he assume that the police would be looking for him? It turns out he was due in court that morning on a minor traffic offense. The reference he makes to "my fault," likely refers to the marital problems his wife admitted they were having.

So if Seabrook rejects "Big John" as a suspect, who does he think was Jack the Stripper? Seabrook believes another former police officer to be the killer, a younger man than "Big John" who also had reason to hold a grudge against the police.

Seabrook's suspect was dismissed from the force in the early 1960s after being convicted of a series of burglaries in the area he patrolled. His motive for the murders was similar to the one Du Rose put forward for "Big John" - to humiliate the police by committing crimes that they would not be able to solve. Seabrook backs up his claim by pointing out that the last six bodies (Elizabeth Figg and Gwynneth Rees were never officially considered part of the series) were each found in different police sub-divisions. Very few people would be aware of these jurisdictions, other than a police officer. Seabrook's suspect had worked in all but one of them.

But even if Seabrook is correct, how does he explain why this suspect suddenly stopped killing? According to Seabrook, the old London police boundaries were changed in April 1965, thus removing his motive. This theory fails to convince. A serial killer, particularly one with at least six murders behind him, rarely stops killing of his own accord, and certainly not for such an arbitrary reason.

More than half a century since the first body turned up on the banks of the Thames, Jack the Stripper, like his infamous namesake, remains a phantom.

*For more True Crime books by Robert Keller please visit*

*http://bit.ly/kellerbooks*

Printed in Great Britain
by Amazon